DK

NORWEGIAN
PHRASE BOOK

A Dorling Kindersley Book

Dorling **DK** Kindersley

LONDON, NEW YORK, SYDNEY, DELHI, PARIS,
MUNICH and JOHANNESBURG

www.dk.com

Compiled by Lexus Ltd with Ragne Hopkins and Helen M Corlett
Printed and bound in Italy by Printer Trento Srl.

First published in Great Britain in 1998
by Dorling Kindersley Limited
9 Henrietta Street, London WC2E 8PS

Reprinted with corrections 2000
2 4 6 8 10 9 7 5 3 1

Dorling Kindersley books can be purchased in bulk quantities at
discounted prices for use in promotions or as premiums. We are
also able to offer special editions and personalized jackets, corporate
imprints, and excerpts from all of our books, tailored specifically to
meet your own needs. To find out more, please contact: Special Sales,
Dorling Kindersley Limited, 9 Henrietta Street, Covent Garden,
London WC2E 8PS; Tel. 020 7753 3572.

A CIP catalogue record is available from the British Library.

ISBN 0 7513 1108 1

Picture Credits

Jacket (front): Corbis Images: Paul Almasy left; Richard T Nowitz
centre, bottom left; Fritz Polking; Frank Lane Picture Agency
spine top; Chris Rainier top right; Adam Woolfitt centre right below,
back cover left; Leslie Garland: top left centre, back cover right;
Robert Harding Picture Library: Kim Hart centre right;
Ghigo Roli bottom right.

CONTENTS

Preface	4
Introduction	5
Useful Everyday Phrases	7
Days, Months, Seasons	14
Numbers	15
Time	16
Hotels	19
Camping and Caravanning	25
Driving	29
Rail Travel	37
Air Travel	45
By Bus, Tram and Boat	49
Eating Out	53
Menu Guide	58
Shopping	71
At the Hairdresser	77
Sport	80
Post Offices and Banks	85
Communications	89
Health	94
Conversion Tables	101
Mini-dictionary	104

PREFACE

This *Dorling Kindersley Travel Guides Phrase Book* has been compiled by experts to meet the general needs of tourists and business travellers. Arranged under headings such as Hotels, Driving and so forth, the ample selection of useful words and phrases is supported by a 2,000-line mini-dictionary. There is also an extensive menu guide listing approximately 450 dishes or methods of cooking and presentation.

Typical replies to questions you may ask during your journey, and the signs or instructions you may see or hear, are shown in tinted boxes. In the main text, the pronunciation of Norwegian words and phrases is imitated in English sound syllables. The Introduction gives basic guidelines to Norwegian pronunciation.

Norway has two languages, **bokmål** and **nynorsk**. Though to some degree different, both languages are understood throughout the whole country. We have used **bokmål** in this phrase book, as it is spoken by the majority of Norwegians.

Dorling Kindersley Travel Guides are recognised as the world's best travel guides. Each title features specially commissioned colour photographs, cutaways of major buildings, 3-D aerial views and detailed maps, plus information on sights, events, hotels, restaurants, shopping and entertainment.

Dorling Kindersley Travel Guides titles include:

Amsterdam · Australia · Sydney · Berlin · Budapest · California
Florida · Hawaii · New York · San Francisco & Northern California
Canada · France · Loire Valley · Paris · Provence · Great Britain
London · Ireland · Dublin · Scotland · Greece: Athens & the Mainland
The Greek Islands · Istanbul · Italy · Florence & Tuscany
Milan & the Lakes · Naples · Rome · Sardinia · Sicily
Venice & the Veneto · Jerusalem & the Holy Land · Mexico · Moscow
St Petersburg · Portugal · Lisbon · Prague · South Africa
Spain · Barcelona · Madrid · Seville & Andalusia · Thailand
Vienna · Warsaw

INTRODUCTION

PRONUNCIATION

When reading the imitated pronunciation, stress that part which is underlined. Pronounce each syllable as if it formed part of an English word and you will be understood sufficiently well. Remember the points below, and your pronunciation will be closer to the correct Norwegian.

EW	try to say 'ee' with your lips rounded (or the French 'u')
HY	the 'hu' sound as in 'huge'
I	the 'i' sound as in 'high'
ow	as in 'cow'
ur	the 'u' sound as in 'fur'

NORWEGIAN ALPHABETICAL ORDER

In the lists called *Things You'll See* and in the Menu Guide we have followed Norwegian alphabetical order. The following letters are listed after z: æ, ø, å.

'YOU'

There are two words for 'you': **du** (addressing one person) and **dere** (addressing two or more people). The polite form **De** is seldom used.

GENDERS AND THE DEFINITE/INDEFINITE ARTICLE

Norwegian has three genders for nouns – masculine, feminine and neuter. Since most feminine words can also have a masculine form, in this phrase book we have mainly used masculine and neuter forms, giving only essential feminine ones.
   The definite article (English 'the') is used as an ending in Norwegian and shows the gender of the noun: **-en** (masculine), **-et** (neuter).Where used, **-a** is the feminine word ending.

When you see translations given in the form **gutt(en)** or **hus(et)**, the form **gutten** will mean 'the boy' and **huset** 'the house'. Note that the final **-t** of the definite article ending is always silent: **huset** _hoosseh_. The indefinite article ending (English 'a', 'an') is the same as the definite article but is placed before the noun as a separate word: **en** or **et**. For example, 'a boy' is **en gutt** and 'a house' is **et hus**.

VERBS

Verbs are given in the infinitive form: '(to) speak' (**å**) **snakke**. To form the present tense for all persons add 'r' to the infinitive: **jeg snakker** 'I speak', **du snakker** 'you speak' and so on.

USEFUL EVERYDAY PHRASES

Yes/no
Ja/nei
yah/nɪ

Thank you
Takk
takk

No, thank you
Nei takk
nɪ takk

Yes, please
Ja takk
yah takk

Please *(offering)*
Vær så god
varshawg<u>o</u>

I don't understand
Jeg forstår ikke
yɪ forsht<u>aw</u>r <u>i</u>kkeh

Do you speak English/French/German?
Snakker du engelsk/fransk/tysk?
sn<u>a</u>kker doo <u>e</u>ng-elsk/fransk/tɛwsk

I can't speak Norwegian
Jeg snakker ikke norsk
yɪ sn<u>a</u>kker <u>i</u>kkeh norshk

I don't know
Jeg vet ikke
yɪ vayt ikkeh

Please speak more slowly
Kan du snakke langsommere
kan doo snakkeh lang-sawmereh

Please write it down for me
Kan du skrive det opp for meg?
kan doo skreeveh deh op for mɪ

My name is …
Jeg heter …
yɪ hayter

How do you do, pleased to meet you
God dag, hyggelig å hilse på deg
go dahg hɛwgeli aw hilseh paw dɪ

Good morning/good afternoon/good evening
God mor'n/god dag/god kveld
go-mawrn/go-dahg/go-kvell

Good night *(when leaving late at night/at bedtime)*
God natt
go-natt

Goodbye
Morn'a; *(informal)* ha det
morna; hah-deh

Excuse me, please
Unnskyld
oonshɛwl

Sorry!
Om forlatelse!
om forl<u>ah</u>delseh

I'm really sorry!
Jeg er virkelig lei meg!
y<small>I</small> ar v<u>i</u>rkeli l<small>I</small> m<small>I</small>

Can you help me?
Kan du hjelpe meg?
kan doo y<u>e</u>lpeh m<small>I</small>

Can you tell me …?
Kan du si meg …?
kan doo see m<small>I</small>

Can I have …?
Kan jeg få …?
kan y<small>I</small> faw

I would like a …
Jeg vil gjerne ha en/et …
y<small>I</small> vil y<u>a</u>rneh hah ayn/et

I would like to …
Jeg vil gjerne …
y<small>I</small> vil y<u>a</u>rneh

Would you like a …?
Vil du ha en/et …?
vil doo hah ayn/et

Is there … here?
Er det … her?
ar deh … har

Where can I get …?
Hvor kan jeg få …?
vohr kan yı faw

How much is it?
Hvor mye koster det?
vohr m_EW_-eh k_o_ster deh

What time is it?
Hvor mange er klokken?
vohr m_a_ng-eh ar kl_o_kken

I must go now
Jeg må gå nå
yı maw gaw naw

I've lost my way *(on foot)*
Jeg har gått meg bort
yı hahr gawt mı bohrt

Cheers!
Skål!
skawl

Do you take credit cards?
Tar du kredittkort?
tahr doo kred_i_ttkort

Where is the British/US embassy?
Hvor er den britiske/amerikanske ambassade?
vohr ar den br_i_tteeskeh/amayreek_ah_nskeh _a_mbassadeh

Where is the toilet?
Hvor er toalettet?
vohr ar toh-a-l_e_tteh

Excellent!
Fint!
feent

**I've lost my passport/money/room key/traveller's cheques/
credit cards**
Jeg har mistet /mitt pass/mine penger/nøkkelen til rommet
mitt/mine reisesjekker/mine kredittkort
*yı hahr meestet /mıtt pass/meeneh peng-er/nurkel-en til rohm-eh
mıtt/meeneh ray-seh-shekker/meeneh kredıttkort*

THINGS YOU'LL HEAR

akkurat	exactly
bare bra, takk	very well, thank you
– og med deg	– and you?
bare hyggelig!	you're welcome!
bra	good
det er riktig	that's right
fint	fine
god dag, hyggelig å hilse på deg	how do you do, nice to meet you
god tur	have a good trip
hei!	hello!; cheerio!
hils …!	regards to …!
hva?	pardon?; sorry?
hva sa du?	sorry, what did you say?
hvordan går det?	how are things?
hvordan har du det?	how are you?
ja	yes
jaså?	is that so?
jeg forstår ikke	I don't understand
jeg vet ikke	I don't know
kom inn	come in
morn'a	cheerio

→

11

nei	no
om forlatelse!	I'm so sorry!
pass deg!	look out!
takk	thanks
takk for i går	literally *'thank you for yesterday'* – greeting used when meeting the day after being together socially or to thank host of party, meal, outing etc.
takk for sist	*'thank you for when we were together last'* (used as **takk for i går** above when more than a day has passed)
takk i like måte	thank you, the same to you
tusen takk	thank you very much
unnskyld	excuse me
velkommen	welcome
vi ses	see you later
vær så god	here you are; on you go; please help yourself

THINGS YOU'LL SEE

1. etg.	ground floor
2. etg.	first floor
damer	women
ferielukning	holiday closing times; closed for holidays
forbudt	forbidden
fullt	full
gate	street
gatekjøkken	snack bar
gratis adgang	admission free
heis	lift
herrer	men

→

ikke	not
informasjon	information
ingen …	no …
ingen adgang	no admittance
inn	way in
inngang	entrance
kasse	cash desk
kvinner	women
lukket	closed
ned	down
nymalt	wet paint
nødutgang	emergency exit
opp	up
opptatt	engaged
politi	police
rabatt	discount, reduction
reservert	reserved
ro	quiet
rom til leie	room to let
salg	sale
skyv	push
stengt	closed
stille	silence
tilbud	special offer
til salgs	for sale
toaletter	toilets
trekk	pull
turistinfo	tourist information
utgang	way out
utsalg	sale
utsolgt	sold out
veg	road
vei	road
åpen	open
åpningstid	opening times

DAYS, MONTHS, SEASONS

Sunday	søndag	*s<u>u</u>rndag*
Monday	mandag	*m<u>a</u>ndag*
Tuesday	tirsdag	*t<u>ee</u>rssdag*
Wednesday	onsdag	*<u>oh</u>nssdag*
Thursday	torsdag	*t<u>aw</u>rssdag*
Friday	fredag	*fr<u>ay</u>dag*
Saturday	lørdag	*l<u>u</u>rrdag*

January	januar	*yanoo-<u>ah</u>r*
February	februar	*febroo-<u>ah</u>r*
March	mars	*marsh*
April	april	*apr<u>ee</u>l*
May	mai	*m<u>i</u>*
June	juni	*y<u>oo</u>ni*
July	juli	*y<u>oo</u>li*
August	august	*owg<u>oo</u>st*
September	september	*sept<u>e</u>mber*
October	oktober	*okt<u>aw</u>ber*
November	november	*nov<u>e</u>mber*
December	desember	*des<u>e</u>mber*

Spring	vår	*vawr*
Summer	sommer	*s<u>o</u>mmer*
Autumn	høst	*hurst*
Winter	vinter	*v<u>i</u>nter*

Christmas	Jul	*yool*
Christmas Eve	Julaften	*y<u>oo</u>laften*
New Year	Nyttår	*n<u>ew</u>tawr*
New Year's Eve	Nyttårsaften	*n<u>ew</u>tawrsaften*
Easter	Påske	*p<u>aw</u>skeh*
Good Friday	Langfredag	*langfr<u>ay</u>dag*
Whitsun	Pinse	*p<u>i</u>nseh*
Midsummer Day	Sankthans	*s<u>a</u>ngt-hanss*

NUMBERS

Compound numbers are found in two forms in Norwegian. The newer form puts the tens before the units, eg: **tjueen** is 'twenty one'. The older form puts the units first, eg: **enogtyve** literally means 'one and twenty'. The old system is still used by many Norwegians and some people use a mixture of both systems.

0	null *nooll*	10	ti *tee*
1	en (ett*) *ayn (ett)*	11	elleve *elveh*
2	to *toh*	12	tolv *tawll*
3	tre *tray*	13	tretten *tretten*
4	fire *feereh*	14	fjorten *fyohrten*
5	fem *fem*	15	femten *femten*
6	seks *seks*	16	seksten *sisten*
7	sju/syv *shoo/sEWv*	17	sytten *surtten*
8	åtte *awtteh*	18	atten *atten*
9	ni *nee*	19	nitten *neetten*

20	tjue/tyve *Hyoo-eh/tEWveh*
21	tjueen/enogtyve *Hyoo-eh-ayn/ayn-aw-tEWveh*
22	tjueto/toogtyve *Hyoo-eh-toh/toh-aw-tEWveh*
30	tretti/tredve *tretti/tredveh*
40	førti/førr *furrti/furr*
50	femti *femti*
60	seksti *seksti*
70	sytti *surtti*
80	åtti *awtti*
90	nitti *neetti*
100	(ett) hundre *hoondreh*
110	hundre og ti *hoondreh aw tee*
200	to hundre *toh hoondreh*
300	tre hundre *tray hoondreh*
400	fire hundre *feereh hoondreh*
1,000	(ett) tusen *toossen*
10,000	ti tusen *tee toossen*
100,000	hundre tusen *hoondreh toossen*
1,000,000	(en) million *milliyohn*

*ett is the neuter form of en

TIME

today	i dag	*ee-dahg*
yesterday	i går	*ee-gawr*
tomorrow	i morgen	*ee-mawern*
the day before yesterday	i forgårs	*ee-forgawrs*
the day after tomorrow	i overmorgen	*ee-awvermawern*
this week	denne uken	*den-eh ooken*
last week	i forrige uke	*ee forri-eh ookeh*
next week	neste uke	*nest-eh ookeh*
this morning	i morges	*ee-morges*
this afternoon	i ettermiddag	*ee-ettermiddag*
this evening/ tonight	i kveld	*ee-kvell*
yesterday afternoon	i går ettermiddag	*ee-gawr ettermiddag*
last night	i går kveld	*ee-gawr kvell*
tomorrow morning	i morgen tidlig	*ee-mawern teeli*
tomorrow night	i morgen kveld	*ee-mawern kvell*
in three days	om tre dager	*om tray dahger*
three days ago	for tre dager siden	*for tray dahger seeden*
late	sent	*saynt*
early	tidlig	*teeli*
soon	snart	*snahrt*
later on	senere	*saynereh*
at the moment	for øyeblikket	*for oyeblikkeh*
second	sekund(et)	*sekoon*
minute	minutt(et)	*minoott*
one minute	et minutt	*et minoott*
two minutes	to minutter	*toh minootter*
quarter of an hour	et kvarter	*et kvartayr*
half an hour	en halv time	*ayn hal teemeh*

16

three quarters of an hour	tre kvarter	*tray kvartayr*
hour	time(n)	*teemeh*
that day	den dagen	*den dahgen*
every day	hver dag	*var dahg*
all day	hele dagen	*hayleh dahgen*
the next day	neste dag	*nesteh dahg*
week	uke(n)	*ookeh*
month	måned(en)	*mawned*
year	år(et)	*awr*

TELLING THE TIME

Norway conforms to Central European Time, which is one hour in advance of GMT. The Norwegians put their clocks forward by an hour from the end of March until the end of September. When telling the time, it is important to note that, instead of saying 'half past' an hour, the Norwegians refer to the next hour coming, for example: 'half past one' in Norwegian is 'half two'.

Also, the minutes after 'quarter past' and before 'quarter to' the hour are linked to the half hour, for example: for 'twenty past three' the Norwegians would say 'ten to half four' and for 'twenty-five to one' they would say 'five past half one'. The 24-hour clock is used quite commonly in timetables, on radio and television and often when making appointments.

am	om formiddagen	*om formiddagen*
pm	om ettermiddagen	*om ettermiddagen*
one o'clock	klokken ett	*klokken ett*
ten past one	ti over ett	*tee awver ett*
quarter past one	kvart over ett	*kvart awver ett*
twenty past one	ti på halv to	*tee paw hal toh*
twenty-five past one	fem på halv to	*fem paw hal toh*
half past one	halv to	*hal toh*
twenty-five to two	fem over halv to	*fem awver hal toh*

twenty to two	ti over halv to	*tee awver hal toh*
quarter to two	kvart på to	*kvart paw toh*
ten to two	ti på to	*tee paw toh*
two o'clock	klokken to	*klokken toh*
13.00 (1 pm)	klokken tretten	*klokken tretten*
16.30 (4.30 pm)	seksten tretti	*sisten tretti*
at half past five	klokken halv seks	*klokken hal seks*
at seven o'clock	klokken sju	*klokken shoo*
noon	klokken tolv	*klokken tawll*
midnight	midnatt	*midnatt*

HOTELS

Norwegian hotels are not graded according to a star system as in the UK, but according to price. Most hotels, however, even the cheap ones, are clean and smart. Note that a 'double room' in Norway can mean a room with twin beds or a double bed. Cheaper hotels have a variety of names: **pensjonat, turistheim, turisthotell, fjellstue** or **sommerhotell.** Youth hostels and cabins for hire on campsites are very popular with travellers on a low budget (see Camping and Caravanning p 25). A **Høyfjellshotell** is a mountain hotel at the top end of the market.

A number of hotels in Norway give price reductions to people with a 'Fjord Pass' which can be obtained for a small fee prior to travelling from the Norwegian Tourist Board's office in most European capitals, or at hotels in Norway.

If you want bed and breakfast type accommodation, look for the signs **ROM** or **VÆRELSE** (room). Breakfast is not always included, but self-catering facilities may be available instead. Meal times in hotels are usually as follows: breakfast 7–10.30 am; lunch 12–2.30 or 3 pm; evening meal 6–11 pm. The Norwegian for dinner or evening meal is **middag** – not be confused with English 'midday'. Be prepared to pay high prices for alcoholic drinks in hotels and restaurants.

A service charge of 10–15% is included in hotel bills, but it is customary to tip for any extra services.

USEFUL WORDS AND PHRASES

balcony	balkong(en)	*balkong*
bathroom	bad(et)	*bahd*
bed	seng(en)	*seng*
bedroom	soverom(met)	*saw-verohm*
bill	regning(en)	*rining*
breakfast	frokost(en)	*frohkost*
dining room	spisesal(en)	*spee-seh-sahl*
dinner	middag(en)	*middag*
double bed	dobbeltseng(en)	*dobbeltseng*

double room	dobbeltrom(met)	_dobbeltrohm_
foyer	foyer(en)	_foh-a-yay_
full board	full pensjon	_full pangshohn_
half board	halv pensjon	_hal pangshohn_
head waiter	hovmester(en)	_hawvmester_
hotel	hotell(et)	_hotel_
hotel manager	hotellsjef(en)	_hotelshayf_
key	nøkkel(en)	_nurkel_
lift	heis(en)	_hiss_
lounge	salong(en)	_salong_
lunch	lunsj(en)	_'lunch'_
reception	resepsjon(en)	_resepshohn_
receptionist	resepsjonist(en)	_resepshohnist_
restaurant	restaurant(en)	_restoorang_
room	rom(met)	_rohm_
room service	romservice(n)	_rohm-'service'_
shower	dusj(en)	_doosh_
single room	enkeltrom(met)	_engkeltrohm_
toilet	toalett(et)	_toh-a-lett_
twin room	tomannsrom	_tohmanssrohm_

Have you any vacancies?
Har dere ledige rom?
hahr dereh laydi-eh rohm

I have a reservation
Jeg har reservert rom
yı hahr ressarvayrt rohm

I'd like a single/twin room
Kan jeg få et enkeltrom/tomannsrom?
kan yı faw et engkeltrohm/tohmansrohm

I'd like a room with a bathroom/balcony
Kan jeg få et rom med bad/balkong?
kan yı faw et rohm may bahd/balkong

I'd like a room for one night/three nights/one week
Kan jeg få et rom for en natt/tre netter/en uke?
kan yɪ faw et rohm for ayn natt/tray netter/ayn ookeh

What is the charge per night?
Hva koster det pr. natt?
vah koster deh par natt

Is there a highchair/cot/baby changing room?
Finnes det en barnestol/barneseng/stellerom?
finnes deh ayn barneh-stohl/barneh-seng/stellehrohm

Is there satellite/cable TV in the rooms?
Finnes det satelitt/kabel-TV på rommene?
finnes deh sahtaylitt/kahbel tayh-vayh paw rohmmehneh

Is there wheelchair access?
Er stedet tilgjengelig for rullestolbrukere?
ayr stedeh till-yengehlee for roollehstohl-brookereh

Are there facilities for the disabled?
Er det tilrettelagt for funksjonshemmede?
ayr deh tilretteh-lahgt for foonkshohns-hemmedeh

Are guide dogs allowed?
Er det tillatt med førerhund?
ayr deh tillatt meh furrehr-hoonn

I don't know yet how long I'll stay
Jeg vet ikke hvor lenge jeg vil bli
yɪ vayt ikkeh vohr leng-eh yɪ vil blee

When is breakfast/lunch/dinner?
Når er frokost/lunsj/middag?
nawr ar frohkost/lunch/middag

Would you have my luggage brought up?
Kan du få bragt opp bagasjen?
kan doo faw brakt op bagahshen

Please wake me at 7 o'clock
Kan du vekke meg klokken sju
kan doo vekkeh mı klokken shoo

Can I have breakfast in my room?
Kan jeg få frokost på rommet?
kan yı faw frohkost paw rohmeh

Can you warm this bottle/baby food for me?
Kan du varme denne flasken/barnematen for meg?
kan doo varmeh denneh flasken/barnehmahten for mı

I'll be back at 10 o'clock
Jeg vil være tilbake klokken ti
yı vil var-eh tilbahkeh klokken tee

My room number is 205
Jeg har rom nummer to hundre og fem
yı hahr rohm noommer toh hoondreh aw fem

I'm leaving tomorrow
Jeg reiser i morgen
yı risser ee-mawern

Can I have the bill, please?
Kan jeg få regningen, takk?
kan yı faw rining-en takk

I'll pay by credit card
Jeg betaler med kredittkort
yı betahler may kredittkor

I'll pay cash
Jeg betaler kontant
yı betahler kontant

Can you get me a taxi?
Kan du få tak i en taxi?
kan doo faw tahk ee ayn taxi

Can you recommend another hotel?
Kan du anbefale et annet hotell?
kan doo anbefahleh et ah-ant hotel

THINGS YOU'LL HEAR

Det er dessverre fullt
I'm sorry, we're full

Vi har ingen enkeltrom igjen
We have no single rooms left

Hvor mange netter er det for?
For how many nights?

Kan du fylle ut dette skjemaet?
Please fill in this form

Kan du skrive navnet ditt her?
Please sign your name here

Hvordan vil du betale?
How will you be paying?

Kan du være så snill å betale på forhånd?
Please pay in advance

THINGS YOU'LL SEE

adgang forbudt	no admittance
annen etasje	first floor
bad	bath
damer	women
dobbeltrom	double room
dusj	shower
enkeltrom	single room
frokost	breakfast
full pensjon	full board
fullt	no vacancies
første etasje	ground floor
halv pensjon	half board
heis	lift
herrer	men
ikke-røykere	non-smokers
inngang	entrance
kvinner	women
ledig	vacancies
menn	men
ned	down
nødutgang	emergency exit
opp	up
overnatting	accommodation
regning	bill
rom	room
rom til leie	room to let
røykere	smokers
røyking forbudt	no smoking
røyking tillatt	smoking permitted
skyv	push
spisesal	dining room
trekk	pull
utgang	exit
værelse til leie	room to let

CAMPING AND CARAVANNING

Norway is the ideal place for a camping holiday as there are a large number of campsites all over the country. Most of them also take caravans. A booklet available from the Norwegian Tourist Board in London and from bookshops in Norway lists most campsites and has a useful map.

Due to the risk of forest fires, open fires are generally not allowed between April and September, especially during a dry summer. You may camp on any ground that is not enclosed, provided you are at least 150 metres from a house or cabin and you leave the site litter-free. If you wish to camp in a field, you need the farmer's permission. Camping is not allowed in roadside picnic areas.

A number of campsites have good camping cabins (**hytter**) and many are open all year round for skiers. The cabins are simple, but clean and comfortable and are usually equipped with a cooker, a fridge, a table and chairs in addition to the bunks for 4–6 people. Take your own pans, crockery, washing-up equipment as well as, of course, sleeping bags. You are expected to leave the cabin clean and tidy and you will be supplied with floor-washing equipment.

Norwegian youth hostels (**vandrerhjem** or **ungdomsherberger**) can be recommended for people of all ages as they are clean and comfortable, and family or twin rooms are often available. It's a good idea to take your own sheets or a sheet-sleeping bag, but if necessary you can hire them from the youth hostel. In the mountains, there are several tourist hostels (**turisthytter**) which are similar to youth hostels. You need to take your own sleeping bag. It's best to book your cabin or hostel in advance if you are going to be arriving late at night.

Be warned that some campsites and hostels, especially in remote areas, may have dry outside toilets called **utedo** – they're nice and clean, but bring a clothes peg for your nose!

Driving with a caravan may be difficult on some roads in the west (see Driving p 29).

Useful Words and Phrases

blanket	ullteppe(t)	*oolltepp-eh*
to borrow	låne	*lawneh*
bucket	bøtte(n)	*burtteh*
cabin	hytte (hytta)	*hEWtteh (hEWtta)*
campfire	bål(et)	*bawl*
to go camping	campe	*kampeh*
camping gas	propangass(en)	*propahngass*
camping permit	camping pass(et)	*kamping pass*
campsite	campingplass(en)	*kampingplass*
caravan	campingvogn	*kampingvongn*
caravan site	campingplass(en)	*kampingplass*
	for campingvogner	*for kampingvongner*
charge	avgift(en)	*ahv-yift*
cooking utensils	kokeutstyr(et)	*kohkeh-ootstEWr*
cutlery	bestikk(et)	*bestikk*
drinking water	drikkevann(et)	*drikkehvann*
electricity	elektrisitet(en)	*elektrisitayt*
firewood	ved(en)	*vay*
groundsheet	teltunderlag(et)	*teltoonerlag*
to hitchhike	haike	*hikeh*
kitchen	kjøkken(et)	*Hyurkken*
rope	tau(et)	*tow*
rubbish	søppel(et)	*surppel*
rucksack	ryggsekk(en)	*rEWgsek*
saucepan	kjele(n)	*Hyayleh*
sheet-sleeping bag	lakenpose(n)	*lahkenpoh-seh*
shop	butikk(en)	*booteekk*
sink	oppvaskbenk(en)	*oppvaskbenk*
sleeping bag	sovepose(n)	*saw-vepoh-seh*
tent	telt(et)	*telt*
trailer	tilhenger(en)	*tilhenger*
youth hostel	vandrerhjem(met)	*vandrer-yem*

Can I camp here?
Kan jeg campe her?
kan yı kampeh har

Can we park the caravan here?
Kan vi parkere campingvognen her?
kan vee parkayreh kampingvongnen har

Where is the nearest campsite/caravan site?
Hvor er nærmeste campingplass?
vohr ar narmesteh kampingplass

What is the charge per night?
Hvor mye koster det pr. natt?
vohr mEweh koster deh par natt

Can I light a fire here?
Kan jeg brenne bål her?
kan yı brenneh bawl har

Where can I get …?
Hvor kan jeg få …?
vohr kan yı faw

Is there drinking water here?
Er det drikkevann her?
ar deh drikkehvann har

Where is/are …?
Hvor er …?
vohr ar

THINGS YOU'LL SEE

brann	fire
bål	campfire
campingplass	campsite
campingvogn	caravan
drikkevann	drinking water
dusj	shower
forbudt	forbidden
forbudt å gjøre opp ild	no campfires
identitetskort	identity card
ild	fire
ingen adgang	no admittance
ingen camping	no camping
kjøkken	kitchen
lys	light
opplysninger	information
pris	price
toalett	toilet
turisthytte	tourist hostel
ungdomsherberge	youth hostel
vandrerhjem	youth hostel
vaskerom	washroom

DRIVING

A driving holiday is one of the best ways to view the spectacular Norwegian scenery. Road-building is difficult and expensive and, on the whole, the roads are narrower and more winding than in Britain, so drive carefully. A number of tunnels have been built through the mountains, and in the highland areas sheep and goats sometimes shelter in the openings in bad weather. Also, watch out for elk crossing the road in forest areas. You will find more toll roads (**bomveg**) in Norway because road-building is so expensive. When you plan your route, you should allow extra time for slower driving as you won't cover as many miles per hour as you would on British roads. Some roads in the west are unsuitable for caravans, so enquire locally about an alternative route. A number of roads in the west and north are linked by car ferries (**bilferge**), and you should allow extra time and money for this. Booking is usually not necessary.

General rules of the road are that you drive on the right, and only roads showing a yellow diamond sign have right of way. On all other roads you have to give way to traffic coming from the right. There may be no stop or give-way sign or even a line to show this. At a roundabout, give way to vehicles that are already on it.

It is compulsory to drive with dipped headlights on at all times, even during the day; to wear seat belts in the front and back of the car; and to carry a warning triangle in case of breakdown. The speed limit on country roads is 80 kph/50 mph and in built-up areas it's 50 kph/30 mph. All other speed limits are signposted in kilometres. It is very important to keep an eye on the speedometer while driving in Norway and to watch out for the speed limit signs. The police have frequent spot checks and automatic monitors (**automatisk trafikk-kontroll**) are in operation where signposted. You may be fined heavily on the spot for speeding. It is also an offence to drive, even a short distance, without your driving licence and vehicle registration documents.

Warning: Do *not* have even one drink and drive in Norway. The police carry out frequent checks, especially at weekends, and the penalty for being over the limit, which is *very low*, is loss of licence and imprisonment!

Petrol stations are scarcer in Norway than in Britain, especially in country and mountain areas, so make sure you have enough petrol for long journeys. Most are self-service stations (**selvbetjening**). They are generally open from 8 am to 9 pm, but some close at midnight. Lead-free petrol (**blyfri**) and 4-star (**98-oktan/super**) are available everywhere

Car hire (**bilutleie**) is quite expensive in Norway.

SOME COMMON ROAD SIGNS

automatisk trafikk-kontroll	automatic speed monitor
begrenset parkering	restricted parking
bomveg	toll road
dårlig veidekke	uneven road surface
enveiskjøring	one-way street
fare	danger
farlig sving	dangerous bend
ferist	cattle grid
fylke	county
gågate	pedestrian precinct
gårdstun	farmyard
jernbaneovergang	level crossing
kjør sakte	drive slowly
kommune	municipality
motorvei	motorway
møteplass	passing place
omkjøring	diversion
parkering	car park
rundkjøring	roundabout
sentrum	town centre

→

turistinfo	tourist information	
ulykkespunkt	accident blackspot	
veiarbeid	roadworks	
veikryss	road junction	

USEFUL WORDS AND PHRASES

automatic	automatisk	*owtohmahtisk*
boot	bagasjerom(met)	*bagahsherohm*
brake *(noun)*	brems(en)	*brems*
breakdown	havari(et)	*havaree*
car	bil(en)	*beel*
car ferry	bilferge(n)	*beelfar-geh*
car park	parkeringsplass(en)	*parkayringssplass*
caravan	campingvogn(en)	*kampingvongn*
clutch	clutch(en)	*'clutch'*
crossroads	veikryss(et)	*vIkrEWss*
to drive	kjøre	*Hyurreh*
engine	motor(en)	*mohtohr*
exhaust	eksos(en)	*eksohs*
fanbelt	vifterem(men)	*vifterem*
garage *(for repairs)*	bilverksted(et)	*beelvarkstayd*
gear	gir(et)	*gear*
headlights	frontlys	*frawntlEWs*
junction		
(motorway exit)	avkjøring(en)	*ahvHyurring*
(motorway entry)	innkjøring(en)	*innHyurring*
licence	sertifikat(et)	*sertifikaht*
lorry	lastebil(en)	*lastebeel*
manual *(gear)*	manuell	*manoo-el*
mirror	speil(et)	*spIl*
motorbike	motorsykkel(en)	*mohtohrsEWkkel*
motorway	motorvei(en)	*mohtohrvI*
number plate	nummerskilt(et)	*noommershilt*
petrol	bensin(en)	*ben-seen*
petrol station	bensinstasjon(en)	*ben-seenstashohn*

rear lights	baklys	*bahklEws*
road	vei(en)	*vI*
to skid	skli	*sklee*
spares	reservedeler	*ressarvehdayler*
speed (noun)	fart(en)	*fart*
speed limit	fartsgrense(n)	*fartsgrenseh*
speedometer	speedometer(et)	*speedomayter*
steering wheel	ratt(et)	*ratt*
to tow	taue	*toweh*
traffic lights	trafikklys(et)	*trafeeklEws*
trailer	tilhenger(en)	*tilhenger*
tyre	dekk(et)	*dekk*
van	varebil(en)	*vahreh-beel*
vehicle registration documents	vognkort(et)	*vongnkort*
wheel	hjul(et)	*yool*
windscreen	frontrute(n)	*frawntrooteh*
windscreen wiper	vinduspusser(en)	*vindoosspoosser*

I'd like some petrol/oil/water
Kan jeg få litt bensin/olje/vann?
kan yI faw litt ben-seen/ol-yeh/vann

Fill her up, please!
Full tank, takk!
full tank takk

I'd like 10 litres of petrol
Kan jeg få 10 liter bensin?
kan yI faw tee leeter ben-seen

Would you check the tyres, please?
Kan du kontrollere dekkene?
kan doo kontrohlayreh dekkeneh

Do you do repairs?
Tar du reparasjoner?
tahr doo reparash<u>oh</u>ner

Where is the nearest petrol station/garage for repairs?
Hvor er nærmeste bensinstasjon/bilverksted?
vohr ar n<u>a</u>rmesteh ben-s<u>ee</u>nstashohn/b<u>ee</u>lvarkstayd

How do I get to ...?
Hvordan kommer jeg til ...?
v<u>oh</u>rdan k<u>o</u>mmer y_I til

Is this the road to ...?
Er dette veien til ...?
ar d<u>e</u>tteh v_I-en til

Which is the quickest route to ...?
Hvilken vei er raskest å kjøre til ...?
v<u>i</u>lken v_I ar r<u>a</u>skest aw H<u>y</u>_Urreh til

Can you repair the clutch?
Kan du reparere clutchen?
kan doo repar<u>ay</u>reh clutchen

DIRECTIONS YOU MAY BE GIVEN

annen til venstre	second on the left
forbi ...	past the ...
første til høyre	first on the right
kjør til høyre	go right
kjør til venstre	go left
på høyre hånd	on the righthand side
på venstre hånd	on the lefthand side
rett fram	straight on

How long will it take?
Hvor lang tid vil det ta?
vohr lang teed vil deh tah

Where can I park?
Hvor kan jeg parkere?
vohr kan yı parkayreh

Can I park here?
Kan jeg parkere her?
kan yı parkayreh har

There is something wrong with the engine
Det er noe galt med motoren
deh ar no-eh galt may mohtohren

The engine is overheating
Motoren blir for varm
mohtohren bleer for varm

I need a new tyre
Jeg trenger et nytt dekk
yı treng-er et nɛwt dekk

I'd like to hire a car
Kan jeg få leie en bil?
kan yı faw lı-eh ayn beel

Is there a mileage charge?
Er det kilometeravgift?
ar deh Hyeelohmayter-ahvyift

Can we hire a baby/child seat?
Kan vi leie et barnesete?
kan vee lay-eh ett barnehsayteh

Things You'll See

92-oktan	2-star
96-oktan	3-star
98-oktan	4-star
angreknapp	cancel
avgift kr. 4 pr. time	charge: 4 kroner an hour
avgiftsbelagt tid 8–17	charge for parking from 8 am to 5 pm
bensin	petrol
bensinstasjon	petrol station
bilverksted	car repairs, garage
blyfri	unleaded
for lite olje	not enough oil
innkjøring	entrance
legg i mynt	insert coin
luft	air
lufttrykk	tyre pressure
maks tid 2 timer	maximum time 2 hours
olje	oil
P-hus	multi-storey car park
parkometer	parking meter
redningstjeneste	breakdown service
reparasjon	repair
returmynt	returned coins
stengt	closed
super	4-star
trykk for billett	press for ticket
utkjøring	exit
vask	car wash
åpen	open

THINGS YOU'LL HEAR

Vil du ha en bil med automatisk eller manuelt gir?
Would you like an automatic or a manual?

Kan jeg få se sertifikatet/vognkortet?
May I see your licence/vehicle registration documents?

RAIL TRAVEL

Rail travel is comfortable and pleasant. The trains are also very clean. Although it is generally more expensive to travel by train in Norway than in Britain (the cost of a return ticket is the same as two singles), there are often reductions and special offers (**tilbud**) available. Senior citizens over the age of 67 should ask for a **Honnørbillett** (*honurrbillett*) – which is a reduced price ticket. A **ScanRail** ticket gives you unlimited travel in Norway, Denmark and Sweden for 21 days.

Some of the routes go through areas of great scenic beauty, and if you are travelling on the main Bergen to Oslo line, it's worth stopping off at Myrdal to take a trip on the mountain railway to Flåm. This route goes through 20 tunnels and in between these you can see some of Norway's most spectacular scenery. In Bergen, there is a funicular railway – **Fløibanen** (*floybahnen*) – to the top of Mount Fløyen where you get a splendid view. Railway enthusiasts may wish to go on the old narrow track train **Tertitten** (*tartitten*) at Sørumsand about 40 km east of Oslo. It runs on Sundays from mid-June to mid-September.

USEFUL WORDS AND PHRASES

adult	(en) voksen	*voksen*
aisle seat	midtgangsplass(en)	*mitgangssplass*
arrival	ankomst	*ankomst*
booking office	billettkontor(et)	*billettkontohr*
buffet car	spisevogn(en)	*speessehvongn*
carriage	vogn(en)	*vongn*
child	barn(et)	*barn*
compartment	kupé(en)	*koopay*
connection	forbindelse(n)	*forbinnelseh*
departure	avgang	*ahvgang*
engine	lokomotiv(et)	*lohkohmohteev*
entrance	inngang(en)	*in-gang*
exit	utgang(en)	*ootgang*

to get on	gå på	*gaw paw*
to get off	gå av	*gaw ahv*
guard	konduktør(en)	*kohndookturr*
indicator board	oppslagstavle for togtider	*oppslagsstavleh for tawgteeder*
left luggage office	reisegodskontor(et)	*rissegoodss-kontohr*
lost property office	hittegodskontor(et)	*hittegoodss-kontohr*
luggage lockers	oppbevaringsbokser	*oppbevahringss-bokser*
luggage trolley	bagasjevogn(en)	*bagahshevongn*
non-smoking	ikke-røykere	*ikkeh roykereh*
platform	plattform(en)	*platform*
reduction	rabatt(en)	*rabatt*
rail, railway	jernbane(n)	*yarnbahneh*
reserved seat	reservert plass	*ressarvayrt plass*
return ticket	returbillett(en)	*retoorbillett*
seat	plass(en)	*plass*
seat reservation	plassbestilling(en)	*plassbestilling*
single ticket	enkeltbillett(en)	*engkeltbillett*
sleeping car	sovevogn(en)	*sawvehvongn*
smoking	røykekupé	*roykehkoopay*
station	stasjon(en)	*stashohn*
station master	stasjonsmester(en)	*stashohns-mester*
ticket	billett(en)	*billett*
ticket collector	konduktør(en)	*kohndookturr*
timetable	togtabell(en)	*tawgtabell*
tracks	spor(et)	*spohr*
train	tog(et)	*tawg*
waiting room	venterom(met)	*venterohm*
window	vindu(et)	*vindoo*
window seat	vindusplass(en)	*vindoossplass*

When does the train for Geilo leave?
Når går toget til Geilo?
nawr gawr tawgeh til yllo

When does the train from Stavanger arrive?
Når kommer toget fra Stavanger?
nawr kommer tawgeh frah Stavanger

When is the next train to Flåm?
Når går neste tog til Flåm?
nawr gawr nesteh tawg til flawm

When is the first train to Trondheim?
Når går første tog til Trondheim?
nawr gawr furrshteh tawg til trawnhɪm

When is the last train to Kristiansand South?
Når går siste tog til Kristiansand S?
nawr gawr sisteh tawg til kristian-sann ess

What is the fare to Gjøvik?
Hvor mye koster en billett til Gjøvik?
vohr mEW-eh koster ayn billett til yurveek

Do I have to change?
Må jeg bytte tog?
maw yɪ bEWteh tawg

Does the train stop at Tønsberg?
Stopper toget i Tønsberg?
stopper tawgeh ee turnssbarg

How long does it take to get to Myrdal?
Hvor lang tid tar det å reise til Myrdal?
vohr lang teed tahr deh aw risseh til mEWrdahl

A single/return ticket to Skien, please
Kan jeg få en enkeltbillett/returbillett til Skien?
kan yɪ faw ayn engkeltbillett/retoorbillett til shay-en

Do I have to pay a supplement?
Må jeg betale ekstra?
maw yɪ betahleh ekstra

I'd like to reserve a seat
Kan jeg få bestille plass?
kan yɪ faw bestilleh plass

Is there a reduction for children?
Gir du/avslag for barn/barnepris?
yeer doo/avslahg for barn/barneh-prees

Do we have to pay for the children?
Må vi betale for barna?
maw vee betaleh for barnah

Is there a family ticket available
Finnes det familie rabatt/familie billett?
finnes deh fahmeelee-eh rahbatt/fahmeelee-eh billett

Is this the right train for Bodø?
Er dette riktig tog til Bodø?
ar detteh rikti tawg til bohdur

Is this the right platform for the Røros train?
Er dette riktig plattform for toget til Røros?
ar detteh rikti platform for tawgeh til rurross

Which platform for the Åndalsnes train?
Hvilken plattform er det for toget til Åndalsnes?
vilken platform ar deh for tawgeh til awndalssnayss

Is the train late?
Er toget forsinket?
ar tawgeh forsinket

Could you help me with my luggage, please?
Kan du hjelpe meg med bagasjen?
kan doo yelpeh mi may bagahshen

Is this a non-smoking compartment?
Er dette en kupé for ikke-røykere?
ar detteh ayn koopay for ikkeh roykereh

Is this seat free?
Er denne plassen ledig?
ar denneh plassen laydi

This seat is taken
Denne plassen er opptatt
denneh plassen ar opptat

I have reserved this seat
Jeg har reservert denne plassen
yi har ressarvayrt denneh plassen

May I open/close the window?
Kan jeg åpne/lukke vinduet?
kan yi awpneh/lookeh vindoo-eh

When do we arrive in Stiklestad?
Når kommer vi til Stiklestad?
nawr kommer vee til stiklehstah

What station is this?
Hvilken stasjon er dette?
vilken stashohn ar detteh

Do we stop at Gol?
Stopper vi i Gol?
stopper vee ee gohl

Is there a buffet car on this train?
Er det spisevogn på dette toget?
ar deh speessehvongn paw detteh tawgeh

Can you tell me where the luggage lockers are?
Kan du si meg hvor oppbevaringsboksene er?
kan doo see mi vohr oppbevahringss-bokseneh ar

THINGS YOU'LL HEAR

Hallo – hallo
Attention

Billetter, takk
Tickets, please

Mosjøen neste. Avstigning på høyre/venstre side
Mosjøen next stop. Get off on the right/left hand side

Kort opphold
Short stop

Togbytte i Drammen
Change trains at Drammen

Toget er ti minutter forsinket
The train is ten minutes late

Toget til Bergen i spor to er klart til avgang
The train to Bergen standing at platform two is ready for
departure

Ta plass!
Please board the train!

Things You'll See

adgang forbudt	no entry
ankomst	arrivals
avgang	departures
aviser og blader	newspapers and magazines
aviskiosk	newspaper kiosk
bagasjeoppbevaring	left luggage
bare ukedager	weekdays only
billetter	tickets
billettkontor	ticket office
drikkevann	drinking water
ekspresstog	express train
forbudt å lene seg ut av vinduet	do not lean out of the window
forsinket	delayed
fraktgods	freight
helligdager	public holidays
hurtigtog	express train
hverdager	weekdays
hver dag unntatt lørdager	everyday except Saturday
informasjon	information
ingen adgang	no entry
inngang	entrance
kun ukedager	weekdays only
ledig	vacant
lokaltog	local train
misbruk er straffbart	penalty for misuse
NSB	Norwegian State Railways
nødbrems	emergency brakes
opptatt	engaged
reise	journey
reisegodsekspedisjon	luggage despatch
reservert	reserved
røykere	smokers

→

røyking forbudt	no smoking
røyking ikke tillatt	smoking not permitted
sentralstasjon	central station
sovevogn	sleeping car
stopper ikke i ...	does not stop at ...
søn- og helligdager	Sundays and public holidays
til togene	to the trains
toaletter	toilets
togtabell	timetable
unntatt søndager	Sundays excepted
utgang	exit
valuta	currency exchange
venterom	waiting room
vogn	carriage

AIR TRAVEL

Regular flights from Britain to Oslo and Stavanger link up with
the domestic network to destinations all over Norway. Look
out for special offers as reductions are often available for
groups and OAPs.

USEFUL WORDS AND PHRASES

aircraft	fly(et)	fl_EW_
air hostess	flyvertinne(n)	fl_EW_vartinneh
airline	flyselskap(et)	fl_EW_selskap
airport	flyplass(en)	fl_EW_plass
airport bus	flybuss(en)	fl_EW_booss
aisle	midtgang	m_i_tgang
arrival	ankomst(en)	_a_nkomst
baggage claim	bagasje- mottakelse(en)	bag_ah_sheh- mohttagelseh
boarding card	boardingkort(et)	'boarding'-kort
to check in	sjekke inn	sh_e_kkeh in
check-in desk	innsjekking(en)	_i_nshekking
customs	toll(en)	tawll
delayed	forsinket	fors_i_nket
departure	avgang(en)	_ah_vgang
departure lounge	avgangshall(en)	_ah_vgangss-hal
emergency exit	nødutgang(en)	n_u_rdootgang
flight	flyrute(n)	fl_EW_rooteh
flight number	flyrute nummer(et)	fl_EW_rooteh n_oo_mmer
gate	utgang(en)	_oo_tgang
jet	jet	yet
to land	lande	l_a_nneh
long-distance flight	langdistansefly(et)	langdist_a_ngsefl_EW_
passport	pass(et)	pass
passport control	passkontroll(en)	p_a_sskontrawl
pilot	flykaptein(en)	fl_EW_kapt_i_n

45

runway	rullebane(n)	*roollehbahneh*
seat	plass(en), sete(t)	*plass, sayteh*
seat belt	sikkerhetsbelte(t)	*sikker-haytsbelteh*
steward	steward(en)	*'steward'*
stewardess	flyvertinne(n)	*flewvartinneh*
takeoff *(noun)*	avgang(en)	*ahvgang*
window	vindu(et)	*vindoo*
wing	vinge(n)	*ving-eh*

When is there a flight to Tromsø?
Når går det fly til Tromsø?
nawr gawr deh flew til trohm-sur

What time does the flight to Bodø leave?
Når går flyet til Bodø?
nawr gawr flew-eh til bohdur

Is it a direct flight?
Går flyet direkte?
gawr flew-eh direkteh

Do I have to change planes?
Må jeg bytte fly?
maw yi bewteh flew

When do I have to check in?
Når må jeg sjekke inn?
nawr maw yi shekkeh in

I'd like a single ticket to Kristiansund North
Kan jeg få en enkeltbillett til Kristiansund N
kan yi faw ayn engkeltbillett til kristian-soon enn

I'd like a return ticket to Molde
Kan jeg få en returbillett til Molde
kan yı faw ayn ret__oo__rbillett til m__aw__ldeh

I'd like a non-smoking seat, please
Kan jeg få en plass for ikke-røykere?
kan yı faw ayn plass for __i__kkeh r__oy__kereh

I'd like a window seat, please
Kan jeg få vindusplass?
kan yı faw v__i__ndoossplass

How long will the flight be delayed?
Hvor lenge vil flyet være forsinket?
vohr l__e__ng-eh vil fl__ew__-eh v__a__reh forsinket

Is this the right gate for the … flight?
Er dette riktig utgang for flyet til …?
ar d__e__tteh r__i__kti __oo__tgang for fl__ew__-eh til

Which gate for the flight to …?
Hvilken utgang er det for flyet til …?
v__i__lken __oo__tgang ar deh for fl__ew__-eh til

When do we arrive in …?
Når kommer vi til …?
nawr k__o__mmer vee til

I do not feel very well
Jeg føler meg ikke helt bra
yı f__u__rler mı __i__kkeh haylt brah

THINGS YOU'LL SEE

ankomst	arrivals
avgang	departures, takeoff
bagasjemottagelse	baggage claim
direkte flyrute	direct flight
fest sikkerhetsbeltene	fasten seat belts
fly	flight
flyvertinne	stewardess
forsinket	delayed
ikke-røykere	non-smokers
informasjon	information
innenriks	domestic
innsjekking	check-in
lokaltid	local time
mellomlanding	intermediate stop
nødutgang	emergency exit
passasjerer	passengers
passkontroll	passport control
redningsvest under setet	life jacket under the seat
rutefly	scheduled flight
røyking ikke tillatt	no smoking please
tollkontroll	customs control
utlandet	international
utgang	gate
valuta-veksling	currency exchange

THINGS YOU'LL HEAR

Flyet til Sandefjord er klart til avgang
The flight for Sandefjord is now boarding

Vennligst gå til utgang nummer fem
Please go now to gate number 5

BY BUS, TRAM AND BOAT

There is an extensive network of both local and long-distance
bus services, a number of which are run by Norwegian State
Railways (**NSB**). A luxury coach service runs from Bergen to
Oslo. Norwegian buses tend to be one-man (or woman)
operated and are very clean and smart. There are still trams in
Oslo and there is also an underground service called **T-banen**
or **undergrunnen**.

The nature of the Norwegian coastline, with its many islands
and fjords, and the fact that many places cannot be reached
overland, means that ferries and boats are major forms of
transport. From Oslo, Bergen and Stavanger there are pleasure
boats and local steamers to the islands and fjords nearby. Express
coastal steamers (**Hurtigruten**) run from Bergen to the north
(including the North Cape), calling in at numerous large and
small ports with deliveries and passengers on the way. A lot of
the main roads in the west and north are linked by car ferries.

A trip on Lake Mjøsa on the world's oldest paddle steamer
'Skibladner' (*shibladner*) makes a pleasant outing.

USEFUL WORDS AND PHRASES

adult	(en) voksen	*voksen*
boat	båt(en)	*bawt*
bus	buss(en)	*booss*
bus stop	buss-stopp(en)	*booss-stop*
to change	bytte	*bewtteh*
child	barn(et)	*barn*
coach	buss(en)	*booss*
conductor	konduktør(en)	*kohndookturr*
connection	forbindelse(n)	*forbinnelseh*
driver	sjåfør(en)	*shawfurr*
fare	billett(en)	*billett*
ferry	ferge(n)	*fargeh*
lake	innsjø(en)	*inshur*

network map	rutekart(et)	*rootehkart*
number 5 bus	buss nummer fem	*booss noommer fem*
passenger	passasjer(en)	*passashayr*
port	havn(en)	*havn*
quay	kai(en)	*kı*
river	elv(en)	*elv*
sea	sjø(en)	*shur*
seat	plass(en)	*plass*
ship	båt(en)	*bawt*
station	stasjon(en)	*stashohn*
subway	undergang(en)	*oonnergang*
taxi	taxi(en)	*'taxi'*
terminus	terminal(en)	*tarminahl*
ticket	billett(en)	*billett*
tram	trikk(en)	*trikk*
underground	undergrunn(en)	*oonnergroon*

Where is the nearest underground station?
Hvor er nærmeste undergrunnsstasjon?
vohr ar narmesteh oonnergroonss-stashohn

Where is the bus station?
Hvor er busstasjonen?
vohr ar booss-stashohnen

Where is there a bus stop?
Hvor er det et buss-stopp?
vohr ar deh ett booss-stop

Which buses go to Bygdøy?
Hvilke busser går til Bygdøy?
vilkeh boosser gawr til bEwgdoy

How often do the buses to Troldhaugen run?
Hvor ofte går bussene til Troldhaugen?
vohr ofteh gawr boosseneh til trollhow-en

Would you tell me when we get to the Vigeland park?
Kan du si fra når vi kommer til Vigelandsparken?
kan doo see frah nawr vee kommer til veeggehlannss-par-kehn

Do I have to get off yet?
Må jeg gå av snart?
maw yı gaw ahv snart

How do you get to the Munch Museum?
Hvordan kommer jeg til Munchmuseet?
vohrdan kommer yı til mohngkmoossay-eh

Is it very far?
Er det langt?
ar deh langt

I want to go to Holmenkollen
Jeg skal til Holmenkollen
yı skal til hawlmenkollen

Do you go near the Viking ship museum?
Kjører du i nærheten av Vikingskipene?
Hyurrer doo i nærhayten av veekingsheepeneh

Where can I buy a ticket?
Hvor kan jeg kjøpe billett?
vohr kan yı Hyurpeh billett

Could you open/close the window?
Kan du åpne/lukke vinduet?
kan doo awpneh/lookeh vindoo-eh

Could you help me get a ticket?
Kan du hjelpe meg å kjøpe billett?
kan doo yelpeh mı aw Hyurpeh billett

When does the last bus leave?
Når går siste buss?
nawr gawr sisteh booss

Where can I get a taxi?
Hvor kan jeg få tak i en taxi?
vohr kan yi faw tahk ee ayn taxi

THINGS YOU'LL SEE

avgang	departure
barn	children
billetter	tickets
billettinspektør	ticket inspector
drosje	taxi
drosjestasjon	taxi rank
enmannsbetjent buss	one-man-operated bus
forstyrr ikke føreren	do not disturb the driver
ha betalingen klar	have fare ready
havn	harbour
ingen inngang	no entry
ingen røyking	no smoking
inngang	entrance
inngang foran/bak	entry at the front/rear
klippekort	punch card for several journeys
nødutgang	emergency exit
rute	route
sjåfør	driver
T-banen	underground
terminal	terminus
utgang bak	exit at rear
voksne	adults

EATING OUT

The Norwegian working day is from about 7 am to 3 or 4 pm and mealtimes are therefore quite early, with lunch mid-morning and dinner at about 4 pm. In hotels and restaurants, however, lunch is normally available between 12 and 2.30 and dinner is available all evening. Eating in hotels and restaurants can be quite expensive. However, you can get good-quality inexpensive meals at cafés which have a set menu **dagens rett** (*dahgenss ret*). Meatballs **kjøttkaker** (*Hyurt-kahker*), thick meat stew **brun lapskaus** (*broon lapskowss*) and pork chops with sweet and sour cabbage **svinekoteletter med surkål** (*sveeneh-koteletter may soorkawl*) are popular dishes. A service charge is usually included in the bill and additional tipping is up to you.

Norwegians eat a substantial breakfast **frokost** (*frohkost*) usually consisting of bread, cold meats, cured fish, a variety of jams and brown Norwegian goats' cheese.

Traditional dishes in Norway are plain and prepared from food which can be easily stored, ie salted, cured, smoked and dried. In the past, the staple diet consisted of various kinds of porridge, and soured cream porridge **rømmegrøt** (*rurmegrurt*), served sprinkled with cinnamon and sugar, was eaten on special occasions like Midsummer's Day. Nowadays, you are likely to come across **spekemat** (*spaykehmaht*), which is a selection of cold cured meats, and this might include cured leg of mutton **fenalår** (*faynalawr*) and cured ham **spekeskinke** (*spaykehshinkeh*), usually served with thin crispbread **flatbrød** (*flatbrur*). These, together with sweet and sour salted herring **sursild** (*soorsill*), cured herring **spekesild** (*spaykehsill*), fermented trout **rakørret** (*rahkurret*) and cured salmon **gravlaks** (*grahvlaks*), are traditionally found in the Norwegian buffet **koldtbord** (*kawltbohr*). The **koldtbord** is often accompanied by a small glass of neat potato spirit called **akevitt** (*akevitt*). Traditional Norwegian food is found in tourist spots like open-air museums and hotels in mountain resorts.

Fish is an important part of the diet in Norway and if you are in Bergen you may want to go to the fish market where an abundance of all kinds of fish and seafood is sold. A bag of prawns eaten at the pier makes a nice lunch.

Street stalls called **gatejøkken** (*gahteнyurkken*) are open late and sell hot dogs, hamburgers, etc. Open sandwiches, usually with cheese, cold meat or prawns, are available in most eating places. Waffles **vafler** (*vafler*), served with soured cream and jam, are another Norwegian favourite.

Licensing laws are strict, alcohol prices are high and the state has a monopoly on the sale of alcohol. Bring your duty-free allowance with you, otherwise you may have to buy spirits at the state-owned **Vinmonopolet** at treble the price. Beer is sold at supermarkets but not wine and spirits. **Pils** (*pilss*) lager and **export øl** (*export url*) strong lager are the most popular beers. Norwegian **lagerøl** (*lahgerurl*) generally has a low alcohol content.

USEFUL WORDS AND PHRASES

beer	øl(et)	url
bill	regning(en)	*rıning*
bottle	flaske(n)	*flaskeh*
buffet	koldtbord(et)	*kawltbohr*
cake	kake(n)	*kahkeh*
chef	kokk(en)	*kokk*
children's portion	barneporsjon(en)	*barneporshohn*
coffee	kaffe(n)	*kaffeh*
cup	kopp(en)	*kopp*
fork	gaffel(en)	*gaffel*
glass	glass(et)	*glass*
knife	kniv(en)	*k-neev*
menu	meny(en)	*menEW*
milk	melk(en)	*melk*
open sandwich	smørbrød(et)	*smurrbrur*
plate	tallerken(en)	*tal-arken*

receipt	kvittering(en)	*kvitt<u>ay</u>ring*
schnapps	akevitt(en)	*akev<u>itt</u>*
serviette	serviett(en)	*sarvi-<u>ett</u>*
snack	smårett(en)	*sm<u>aw</u>rett*
soup	suppe(n)	*s<u>oo</u>ppeh*
spoon	skje(en)	*shay*
sugar	sukker(et)	*s<u>oo</u>kker*
table	bord(et)	*bohr*
tea	te(en)	*tay*
teaspoon	teskje(en)	*t<u>ay</u>shay*
tip	tips(et)	*tips*
waiter	kelner(en)	*k<u>e</u>lner*
waitress	serveringsdame(n)	*sarv<u>ay</u>ringssdahmeh*
water	vann(et)	*vann*
wine	vin(en)	*veen*
wine list	vinkart(et)	*v<u>ee</u>nkart*

A table for one/two, please
Kan jeg få et bord til en/to, takk?
kan yɪ faw et bohr til ayn/too takk

Can I see the menu?
Kan jeg få se menyen?
kan yɪ faw say men<u>ew</u>en

Can I see the wine list?
Kan jeg få se vinkartet?
kan yɪ faw say v<u>ee</u>nkarteh

What would you recommend?
Hva vil du anbefale?
vah vil doo <u>ahn</u>befahleh

I'm allergic to nuts/shellfish
Jeg er allergisk mot nøtter/skalldyr
yɪ ar all<u>a</u>rgisk moht n<u>u</u>rttehr/sk<u>a</u>ll-dɛwr

I'm vegetarian
Jeg er vegetarianer
yı ar veggetahreeahnehr

Do you have any vegetarian dishes?
Har dere vegetarretter?
hahr dayreh veggetahr-retter

I'd like …
Kan jeg få …
kan yı faw

Just a cup of coffee, please
Bare en kopp kaffe, takk
bahreh ayn kopp kaffeh takk

Waiter/waitress!
Hallo!
hallo

Can we have the bill, please?
Kan vi få regningen, takk?
kan vee faw rıning-en takk

I only want a snack
Jeg vil bare ha en smårett
yı vil bahreh hah ayn smawrett

Is there a set menu?
Er det en dagens rett?
ar deh ayn dahgenss rett

I didn't order this
Jeg har ikke bestilt dette
yı hahr ikkeh behstilt detteh

Can I have another knife/fork?
Kan jeg få en kniv/gaffel til?
kan yı faw ayn k-neev/gaffel til

May we have some more …?
Kan vi få litt mer …?
kan vee faw litt mayr

The meal was very good, thank you
Maten smakte deilig, takk!
mahten smahkteh dıli takk

Can we pay separately?
Kan vi betale hver for oss?
kan vee betahleh var for oss

THINGS YOU'LL HEAR

Håper det smaker
Enjoy your meal

Hva skal det være å drikke?
What would you like to drink?

Skål!
Cheers!

Smakte det?
Did you enjoy your meal?

Vær så god!
Here you are!

MENU GUIDE

In the Menu Guide we have followed Norwegian alphabetical order. The following letters are listed after z: æ, ø, å.

aftens	evening meal
agurk(er)	cucumber; pickled gherkins
akevitt	clear spirit made from potatoes (drunk neat with food)
alkoholfri(tt)	alcohol-free
and	duck
ananas	pineapple
ansjos	anchovies
appelsin	orange
aprikos	apricot
asparges	asparagus
bakt	baked
banan	banana
bankekjøtt	brown meat and onion stew
barnemeny	children's menu
barneporsjon	children's portion
benløse fugler	veal 'olives' (thin slices of veal stuffed and rolled up)
bernaisesaus	béarnaise sauce (made with butter, egg yolks and spices and served with fried meat)
betasuppe	yellow pea, ham and vegetable soup
biff med løk	fried steak with onions
bjørnebær	blackberries, brambles
blandet kjøttrett	a variety of meats diced and fried
blomkål	cauliflower
bløtkake	cream gâteau
bløtkokt egg	soft-boiled egg
blåbær	blueberries
blåskjell	mussels
boller	buns; dumplings; fish or meatballs
brennevin	spirits
bringebær	raspberries
brokkoli	broccoli
brun(e)	brown

brun lapskaus	beef and potato stew in thick brown gravy
brus	fizzy drinks
bryst	breast
brød	bread
buljong	clear soup, consommé
butterdeig	flaky pastry
bønner	beans
bønnespirer	bean sprouts
chips	potato crisps
dagens	of the day
dampet	steamed
diverse	assorted
drikkevarer	drinks
druer	grapes
dyrestek	roast reindeer
eddik	vinegar
eggedosis	egg nog
eggehvite	egg white
eggekrem	thick custard
eggeplomme	egg yolk
eggerøre	cold scrambled eggs with chives
eksportøl	export beer
elg	elk
eple	apple
eplemos	stewed apples
eplemost	apple juice
erter	peas
erter, kjøtt og flesk	yellow pea soup and ham (with the ham served as the second course with boiled potatoes)
Farris®	mineral water
fasan	pheasant
fenalår	cured leg of mutton
fersken	peach
fersk suppe og kjøtt	vegetable broth and boiled beef (with the beef served as the second course with boiled potatoes and sweet and sour onion sauce)
filet	fillet
fisk(e)	fish
flambert	flambé (served in flaming brandy)

MENU GUIDE

flaske	bottle
flatbrød	'flat bread' (leaf-thin crispbread)
flesk	pork belly
fleskepannekake	ham omelette
flyndre	sole
fløte	cream
fløterand med frukt	cream and vanilla mousse with fruit
forloren	meat loaf served as a roast (mock duck, etc)
forlorent egg	poached egg
formiddagsmat	lunchtime snack
forrett	first course
fransk	French
franskbrød	white bread with poppy seeds
frikassé	fricassee (stewed meat served in a thick white sauce)
frisk(e)	fresh
frityrstekt	deep-fried
frokost	breakfast
frokostblanding	breakfast cereal
fromasj	cold soufflé, mousse
frukt	fruit
fylt	stuffed
får	mutton
fårikål	lamb and cabbage stew with whole peppercorns
gaffelbiter	small fillets of herring soaked in strong marinade
gammelost	'old cheese' (strong, pungent, very low-fat cheese)
garnert	garnished
geitost	sweet, brown Norwegian goats' cheese
gelé	jelly (either sweet or savoury)
glassert(e)	glazed
gløgg	mulled wine
grapefrukt	grapefruit
grape soda	fizzy grapefruit drink
grateng	savoury hot soufflé
gratinert(e)	fried in breadcrumbs
gravlaks	cured salmon (gravad lax)
greddeost	Swedish full-cream cheese
gressløk	chives

griljert	fried in breadcrumbs
grillben	barbecued spareribs
grovbrød	wholemeal bread
gryte	casserole
grønnsaker	vegetables
grøt	porridge made from flour, oats or rice; 'jelly' made from boiled fruit and fruit juice, and thickened with cornflour
gulrot	carrot
gulrøtter	carrots
gås	goose
hakket	chopped
halvtørr	medium dry
hamburgerrygg	smoked loin of pork
hare	hare
hasselnøtter	hazelnuts
havre	oatmeal
hellefisk	halibut
helmelk, helmjølk	full-cream milk
helstekt	fried or roasted whole
hetvin	fortified wine
hjemmelaget	home-made
hoffdessert	'court dessert' (pyramid of meringues with chocolate, whipped cream and flaked almonds)
honning	honey
hovedrett	main course
hummer	lobster
husets	of the house
hvalbiff	whale steak
hveteboller	buns
hvetekake	large bun, served sliced with butter
hvitløk	garlic
hvit saus	white sauce
hvitting	whiting
hvitvin	white wine
høns(e)	chicken, poultry
hårdkokt egg	hard-boiled egg
is	ice cream, ice
iskake	ice cream cake
iskrem	ice cream

italiensk salat	ham, apple, gherkin and vegetable salad in mayonnaise
jordbær	strawberries
juice	fruit juice
julebord	Christmas buffet
kabaret	fish, meat or vegetables in aspic
kaffe	coffee
kakao	cocoa
kake(r)	cake(s); fish or meat cakes
kald	cold
kaldrøkt	cold smoked salmon
kalkun	turkey
kalv(e)	veal
kanel	cinnamon
kanne	tea or coffee pot
kantareller	chanterelles
kapers	capers
kaperssaus	white sauce with capers
karaffel	carafe of wine
karamellpudding med krem	caramel custard with whipped cream
karbonade	minced beef steak
karrisaus	very mild, white curry sauce
karve	caraway seeds
kaviar	caviar; sandwich spread made from cod roe
kavring	rusk
kinakål	Chinese leaves
kirsebær	cherries
kjeks	biscuits
kjøtt	meat
kjøttkaker (med brun saus)	minced beef balls (in a brown gravy)
knakkpølse	small, thick smoked sausage
kneipbrød	crusty wheaten bread
knekkebrød	crispbread
kokt	boiled, poached
koldtbord	cold buffet
kompott	stewed fruit
konfekt	filled chocolates
kotelett	chop, cutlet
krabbe	crab

kransekake	'wreath cake' (almond macaroon rings stacked into a tower and decorated with flags and crackers – often eaten on birthdays)
krem	whipped cream
kreps	crayfish
kringle	pretzel-shaped cake made with yeast and filled with almond paste, apples or raisins
krokan	chopped pieces of caramel with toasted almonds (used in ice cream or as a topping for desserts)
krumkaker	'curved cakes' (crisp cone-shaped cakes)
krydder	spice
kryddersild	cured, spiced raw herring
kulturmelk, kulturmjølk	soured milk
kveite	halibut
kveldsmat	evening meal
kylling	chicken
kål	cabbage
kålrabi, kålrot	swede
kålrulletter	cabbage parcels filled with minced meat and served with a sauce
lagerøl	low-alcohol beer
laks	salmon
lam(me)	lamb
lammerygg	saddle of lamb
lapskaus	beef and potato stew with vegetables
lefse	type of pancake served cold with butter, sugar and cinnamon
leskedrikk	squash
lett	'light' (lightly-cooked, low-fat, low-alcohol or low-sugar)
lettmelk	semi-skimmed milk
lever	liver
light	'diet' (low in sugar or no sugar)
likør	liqueur
loff	white bread
lumpe	thin potato scone eaten with hot dogs
lungemos	mashed lungs and offal eaten hot or cold (similar to haggis)
lunsj	lunch

lutefisk	cod soaked in lye of potash and then served with white sauce and melted butter or with bacon or with mashed peas
løk	onion
lår	leg
mais	sweetcorn
maiskolbe	corn on the cob
majones	mayonnaise
makaroni	macaroni
makrell	mackerel
makron	macaroon
mandel	almond
mandelkjernepudding	almond-flavoured blancmange
marengs	meringues
marinert	marinated
med	with
medisterkaker	fried meatballs made from minced pork
medisterpølse	fried or poached pork sausage
mel	flour
melk	milk
meny	menu
middag	dinner
mineralvann	mineral water; fizzy drinks
mjølk	milk
moreller	cherries
multer	cloudberries (wild orange-coloured berries, similar in shape to blackberries)
multekrem	'cloudberry cream' (whipped cream with cloudberries)
munker	'monks' (ball-shaped doughnuts with jam or apple)
mørbrad	sirloin
napoleonskake	'Napoleon's cake' (custard slice)
naturell	natural; served in the shell (of seafood)
norvegia ost	hard, mild cheese
nygrodde poteter	new potatoes boiled in their skins
nype	rosehip
nypesuppe	rosehip soup (usually served with whipped cream as a dessert)
nyrer	kidneys
nøkkelost	hard cheese with caraway seeds

nøtter	nuts
okse	beef
oksehale	oxtail
okseragu	beef and pork stew with red wine
okserull	belly of beef stuffed, spiced and cured (sliced cold for sandwiches)
oksestek	roast beef
ost	cheese
ostesufflé	cheese soufflé
ost og kjeks	cheese and biscuits
ovnsbakt	oven-baked
panert	coated with breadcrumbs
pannekaker	large thin pancakes
paprika	paprika; red, green or yellow peppers
pariserloff	French stick
peppermynte	peppermint
pepperrot	horseradish
pepperstek	pepper steak
persille	parsley
persillerot	parsnip
pils	lager
pinnekjøtt	salted, dried side of lamb, boiled and served with mashed turnip
pisket krem	whipped cream
pistasj is	pistachio ice cream
platte	platter with selection of cold meat or fish
plomme(r)	plum(s), egg yolk
plukkfisk	poached, salted cod in white sauce
pochert	poached
pommes frites	chips, French fries
portvin	port
postei	pâté, vol-au-vent
poteter	potatoes
potet gull	crisps
pudding	fish or meat loaf; sweet pudding, blancmange
puré	purée
purre	leeks
pytt i panne	fried, diced meat and potatoes, served with a fried egg on top
pære	pear
pølser	frankfurter sausages

pålegg	sandwich spread or cold meat for sandwiches
rabarbra	rhubarb
ragu	stew
rakørret	fermented trout
raspeball	dumpling made from grated potato
reddiker	radishes
reinsdyr	reindeer
reke(r)	prawns
rekesalat	prawn cocktail
rekesaus	white sauce with prawns
remulade	mayonnaise with chopped gherkins and spices
remuladesaus	mayonnaise and whipped cream with spices and chopped gherkins
rett(er)	dish(es), course(es)
reven, revet, revne	grated
ribbe	side of either pork or lamb
rips	redcurrants
ris	rice
risgrøt med smørøye	rice porridge with a knob of butter, served with cinnamon and sugar
riskrem med rød saus	cold rice pudding mixed with whipped cream and served with red berry sauce
rislapper	small rice porridge pancakes eaten hot with jam
ristet	toasted, fried, roast
roastbiff med løk	roast fillet of beef with fried onions
rogn	roe
rosenkål	brussels sprouts
rosiner	raisins
rugbrød	rye bread
rullekake	swiss roll
rundstykke	crusty roll
russisk salat	ham and cooked vegetables in mayonnaise dressing
rype(r)	grouse, ptarmigan
rød	red
rødbeter	beetroot
rødgrøt med fløte	soft red berry 'jelly' with cream
rødkål	sweet and sour boiled red cabbage with caraway seeds

rødspette	plaice
rødvin	red wine
røkelaks	smoked salmon
røket, røkt	smoked
røkt svinekam	smoked loin of pork
rømme	soured cream
rømmegrøt	porridge made from soured cream and white flour, served with cinnamon and sugar (traditional Midsummer dish)
rømmekolle	bowl of soured cream served with toasted breadcrumbs and sugar
rørt(e)	uncooked fruit mixed with sugar
rå	raw
råkostsalat	raw vegetable salad
råkrem	whipped cream with yolks of egg
sadel	saddle
saft	juice, squash
saftsuppe	red fruit juice soup
salat	lettuce; salad; in mayonnaise dressing
saltpølse	salami
sardiner	sardines
saus	sauce
sei	coley
seibiff	fried coley steaks with fried onions
selleri(rot)	celeriac
semulegrøt	semolina pudding served with red fruit sauce
sennep	mustard
service inkludert	service charge included
seterrømme	extra thick soured cream (as made at a 'seter' – a mountain farm)
sild	herring
sildesalat	cured herring salad with beetroot and onion
sitron	lemon
sitronbrus	lemonade
sjampinjong	field mushroom
sjokolade	chocolate
skalldyr	shellfish
skinke	ham
skjell	shells; puff pastry 'shells'
skummet melk/mjølk	skimmed milk
sky	meat juices

slangeagurk	cucumber
smeltet smør	melted butter
smultringer	doughnuts
smør	butter
smørbrød	open sandwich
smørgrøt	porridge made from white flour, served with cinnamon, sugar and a knob of butter
snitter	small open sandwiches
solbær	blackcurrants
Solo*	orangeade
sopp	mushroom
speilegg	fried egg ('sunny side up')
spekemat	tray of various kinds of cured and smoked cold meat and fish (served with 'flatbrød')
spekepølse	salami
spekesild	cured, raw herring
spekeskinke	cured leg of ham
spinat	spinach
spisekart	menu
stangselleri	celery
stappe	mashed
stek	roast
stekt	fried, roasted
stikkelsbær	gooseberries
stuing	in white or cream sauce
sufflé	soufflé
sukker	sugar
sukkererter	mangetout
sukrede rips	redcurrants with sugar
suppe	soup
surkål	sweet and sour boiled cabbage with caraway seeds (sauerkraut)
sur og søt	sweet and sour
sursild	cured pickled herring
svin(e)	pork
svinekam	loin of pork
svisker	prunes
svor	pork crackling
sylte	brawn
sylteflesk	cured and spiced boiled belly of pork
syltet	preserved, pickled

syltetøy	jam
søt	sweet
tartarsaus	mayonnaise with chopped egg, onion, capers and gherkins
tartarsmørbrød	open sandwich with raw beef, raw egg yolk, chopped onion and beetroot
T-benstek	T-bone steak
te	tea
tebriks	puff pastry rolls with poppy seeds
terninger	diced
terte	tart, pastry
tilslørte bondepiker	'farm maids with a veil' (stewed apples with toasted breadcrumbs and whipped cream)
tiur	capercaillie
tomat	tomato
torsk	cod
trollkrem	'troll cream' (whipped cream with egg whites and a sweet cowberry 'tyttebær' sauce)
trøfler	truffles
tunge	tongue
tyttebær	cowberries (like cranberries)
tørr	dry
urter	herbs
urtete	herb tea
vafler	waffles
valnøtter	walnuts
vanilje	vanilla
vaniljesaus	custard sauce
vann	water
vannbakkels	choux pastry cakes filled with whipped cream
varm	warm, hot
varm(e) retter	hot dishes
varme pølser	hot dogs
varm sjokolade med krem	hot chocolate with whipped cream
vegetariansk	vegetarian
vegetarretter	vegetarian dishes
vestkystsalat	shellfish salad
vilt	game
viltsaus	cream sauce (served with game)
vin	wine
vindruer	grapes

vinkart	wine list
vørtekake	large bun, served sliced with butter
vørterøl	sweet alcohol-free or low-alcohol beer
waldorfsalat	Waldorf salad (with apples, celery and walnuts)
waleskringle	choux pastry ring
wienerbrød	Danish pastry
wienerpølser	frankfurter sausages
wienerschnitzel	escalope of veal fried in breadcrumbs
øl	beer
ørret	trout
østers	oysters
ål	eel

SHOPPING

Opening times vary. Shops are generally open from 9 am to 6 pm on weekdays, but close at 3 pm on Saturdays. Some grocery shops may stay open until 10 pm. Shopping centres open around 10 am and close at 9 pm on weekdays and 6 pm on Saturdays.

Although prices tend to be higher in Norway than in Britain, there are often sales and reduced prices – look out for the sign **tilbud** which means 'special offer'.

Popular things for tourists to buy are found in the craft shops (**husflidsforretning**), which sell traditional Norwegian handmade goods like sweaters, pottery, glass, pewter and wooden objects.

A number of shops offer tax-free shopping for tourists – look for the sign (it is always in English). In these shops value-added tax (**moms**) is included as usual, but if your total bill comes to more than 300 kroner, you can claim back 10–15% of the total at the airport or on the ferry when you leave the country. The shop assistant will seal the parcel and complete a form to enable you to do this.

USEFUL WORDS AND PHRASES

baker	bakeri(et)	*bak-eree*
bookshop	bokhandel(en)	*bohkhandel*
butcher	slakter(en)	*slakter*
to buy	kjøpe	*Hyurpeh*
cake shop	konditori(et)	*kohnditohree*
carrier bag	bærepose(n)	*bareh-pohsseh*
cheap	billig	*billi*
chemist	apotek(et)	*apohtayk*
china	porselen(et)	*pawrselayn*
to cost	koste	*kosteh*
craft shop	husflidsforretning(en)	*hoosfleedss-forretning*
department store	varemagasin(et)	*vahremaga-seen*
expensive	dyrt	*dewrt*
fashion	mote(n)	*mohteh*

fishmonger	fiskebutikk(en)	*fiskehbooteekk*
florist	blomsterbutikk(en)	*blomsterbooteekk*
fruit	frukt(en)	*frookt*
furniture	møbler	*murbler*
gift shop	gavebutikk(en)	*gahvehbooteekk*
grocer	dagligvarebutikk(en)	*dahglivahrebooteekk*
ironmonger	jernvarehandel(en)	*yarnvahrehandel*
menswear	herreklær	*harreklar*
newsagent	avis- og	*aveess aw*
	tobakksbutikk(en)	*tohbaksbooteekk*
receipt	kvittering(en)	*kvittayring*
record shop	musikkforretning(en)	*moo-seekkforretning*
sale	salg(et)	*salg*
shoe shop	skobutikk(en)	*skohbooteekk*
shop	butikk(en)	*booteekk*
to go shopping	handle	*hand-leh*
souvenir shop	suvenirbutikk(en)	*sooveneerbooteekk*
to spend	bruke (penger)	*brookeh (peng-er)*
supermarket	supermarked(et)	*soopermarked*
till	kasse(n)	*kasseh*
toy shop	leketøysbutikk(en)	*layketoyss-booteekk*
travel agent	reisebyrå(et)	*rissehbEWraw*
vegetables	grønnsaker	*grurnsahker*
women's wear	dameklær	*dahmeklar*

I'd like …
Jeg skal ha …
yi skal hah

Do you have …?
Har du …?
hahr doo

How much is this?
Hvor mye koster denne (dette)?
vohr mEW-eh koster denneh (dehtteh)

Where is the women's department?
Hvor er dameavdelingen?
vohr ar dahmeh-avdayling-en

Do you have any more of these?
Har du flere av disse?
hahr doo flayreh av deesseh

I'd like to change this, please
Kan jeg få bytte denne (dette)?
kan yı faw bewteh denneh (dehtteh)

Have you anything cheaper?
Har du noe som er billigere?
hahr doo no-eh som ar billi-ereh

Have you anything larger/smaller?
Har du noe som er større/mindre?
hahr doo no-eh som ar sturreh/mindreh

Does it come in other colours?
Har du den i andre farger?
hahr doo den ee andreh farger

Could you wrap it for me?
Kan du pakke den inn for meg?
kan doo pakkeh den in for mı

Can I have a receipt?
Kan jeg få en kvittering?
kan yı faw ayn kvittayring

Can I have a carrier bag, please?
Kan jeg få en bærepose?
kan yı faw ayn barehpoh-seh

Can I try it/them on?
Kan jeg prøve den/dem?
kan yı prurveh den/dem

Where do I pay?
Hvor skal jeg betale?
vohr skal yı betahleh

Can I have a refund?
Kan jeg få pengene igjen?
kan yı faw peng-eneh ee-yen

I'm just looking
Jeg bare ser
yı bahreh sayr

I'll come back later
Jeg kommer tilbake senere
yı kommer tilbahkeh saynereh

THINGS YOU'LL HEAR

Får du?
Are you being served?

Vær så god!
Can I help you?; next please!; here you are!

Kan jeg hjelpe deg?
Can I help you?

Vi har dessverre ikke flere/mer igjen
I'm sorry we're out of stock

$\longrightarrow$

Dette er alt vi har
This is all we have

Var det noe annet?
Will there be anything else?

Skal det være en gave?
Would you like it gift-wrapped?

Det blir åttifem kroner, takk
That will be 85 kroner, please

Har du mindre penger?
Have you anything smaller? (money)

THINGS YOU'LL SEE

annen etasje	first floor
avdeling	department
bakeri	baker's
best før …	best before …
billig	cheap
blomster	flowers
bokhandel	bookshop
brukskunst	crafts
butikk	shop
dagligvarer	groceries
dameklær	women's wear
ferielukning	holiday closing times; closed for holidays
grønnsaker	vegetables
herreklær	menswear
husflidsforretning	craft shop
is/iskrem	ice cream
kalorier	calories

→

kasse	till, checkout
kjøpesenter	shopping centre
konditori	cake shop
kullhydrater	carbohydrates
kvalitet	quality
leketøy	toys
lukket	closed
moms	VAT
mote	fashion
nedsatt	reduced
pant	refund (on bottles)
pelsforretning	fur shop
pris	price
rabatt	reduced
reisebyrå	travel agent
rengjøringsartikler	household cleaning materials
selvbetjening	self-service
skoforretning	shoe shop
slakter	butcher
sommersalg	summer sale
stengt	closed
sukkerfri	sugar-free
tilbud	special offer
tobakksbutikk	tobacconist
underetasje	lower floor
urmaker	watchmaker
utsolgt	sold out
varehus	department store
varemagasin	department store
vennligst ikke rør varene	please do not touch
vennligst ta en vogn/kurv	please take a trolley/basket
vennligst ta kønummer	please take a queue number
vi kan dessverre ikke gi pengene tilbake	we regret we cannot give cash refunds
åpningstider	opening hours

AT THE HAIRDRESSER

Hairdressing standards in Norway are high and so are the prices. At women's hairdressers you will have to make an appointment; at men's salons you can often just drop in.

USEFUL WORDS AND PHRASES

appointment	time(n)	_teemeh_
beard	skjegg(et)	_shegg_
blond	blond	_blonn_
brush	børste(n)	_burrsteh_
comb	kam(men)	_kam_
conditioner	balsam	_balsam_
curlers	hårruller	_hawr-rooller_
curling tongs	krølltang(en)	_krulltang_
curly	krøllete	_krulleteh_
dark	mørkt	_murrkt_
fringe	pannelugg(en)	_panneloogg_
gel	gelé	_shelay_
hair	hår(et)	_hawr_
haircut	hårklipp(en)	_hawrklipp_
hairdresser	frisør(en)	_freesurr_
hairdryer	hårtørrer(en)	_hawrturrer_
hairspray	hårspray(en)	_hawr-'spray'_
highlights	striper	_streeper_
long	langt	_langt_
moustache	bart(en)	_bart_
parting	skill(en)	_shill_
perm	permanent(en)	_parmanent_
setting lotion	leggevann(et)	_leggehvann_
shampoo	sjampo(en)	_shampo_
to have a shave	barberes	_barbayress_
shaving foam	barberskum(met)	_barbayr-skohm_
short	kort	_kort_
styling mousse	hårskum(met)	_hawr-skohm_
wavy	fald	_fal_

I'd like to make an appointment
Kan jeg få bestille time?
kan yɪ faw bestilleh teemeh

I'd like a shampoo/cut and blow-dry/set, please
Jeg skal vaske/klippe og føne/legge håret
yɪ skal vaskeh/klippeh aw furneh/leggeh hawreh

Not too much off
Ikke ta for mye av
ikkeh tah for mEW-eh ahv

A bit more off here, please
Kan du ta litt mer av her?
kan doo tah litt mayr ahv har

I'd like a perm
Jeg skal ta permanent
yɪ skal tah parmanent

I'd like highlights
Jeg vil ha striper
yɪ vill hah streeper

THINGS YOU'LL SEE

barbering	shave
damefrisør	women's salon
fargeskylling	colour rinse
for fett hår	for greasy hair
for tørt hår	for dry hair
frisør	hair stylist, hairdresser
frisørsalong	hairdressing salon
føn	blow-dry
herrefrisør	men's hairdresser
hårlakk	hairspray
leggevann	setting lotion
permanent	perm
toning	tint
vasking og legging	shampoo and set

THINGS YOU'LL HEAR

Hvordan vil du ha det?
How would you like it?

Er det kort nok?
Is that short enough?

Vil du ha balsam?
Would you like any conditioner?

Er det passe?
Is that all right?

SPORT

Norway's coastal areas are excellent for sailing and all kinds of water sports. The weather in the south is often pleasantly hot, and from the Swedish border all along the southern coast there are numerous beaches which are suitable for sunbathing and swimming. Thanks to the Gulf Stream, the water is usually comfortably warm. Sailing, windsurfing, water-skiing and boating are all popular. Norway has many lakes which are good for fishing, especially in the mountains, but you will often need a fishing permit (**fiskekort**). There are also a number of good salmon rivers for which a fishing permit is always required.

Norway has vast mountain areas, Hardangervidda, Rondane and Jotunheimen, with the highest peak, Galdhøpiggen, reaching 2,469 metres (8,100 feet) above sea level. These regions are very popular for hillwalking as there's a good network of paths marked by the Norwegian hillwalking organisation (**Den Norske Turistforening**). This organisation also runs a number of mountain hostels, some of which are basic, but always clean and comfortable – you need to bring a sleeping bag with you. Conducted tours over the mountain glaciers are an interesting experience.

Cycling is another popular summer activity and there are a number of quiet roads and cycle paths suitable for this.

There is a growing interest in Norway in games like tennis, badminton and squash and you will find facilities for these at sports centres and clubs in most towns.

Skiing as a sport originated in Telemark in the second half of the 19th century and is Norway's main winter sport. As most of the country is covered by snow in winter and well into spring, cross-country skiing is possible almost everywhere. Downhill or slalom skiing is centred in the mountain areas where ski tows have been put up in numerous places. Geilo, Gol, Hemsedal and Voss are the biggest and most popular resorts. These places are especially busy during the Easter weekend as the Norwegians traditionally go skiing at this time.

There are good outdoor facilities for skating in the winter when a large number of football stadiums are turned into skating rinks for the public.

USEFUL WORDS AND PHRASES

badminton	badminton	*badminton*
ball	ball(en)	*bal*
beach	strand(en)	*strann*
bicycle	sykkel(en)	*sEWkel*
bindings *(ski)*	bindinger	*binning-ehr*
boat	båt(en)	*bawt*
canoe	kano(en)	*kahnoh*
canoeing	kanopadling(en)	*kahno-padling*
cycle path	sykkelsti(en)	*sEWkelstee*
cycling trip	sykkeltur(en)	*sEWkeltoor*
deck chair	fluktstol(en)	*flooktstohl*
diving board	stupebrett(et)	*stoopehbrett*
to fish	fiske	*fiskeh*
fishing rod	fiskestang(en)	*fiskestang*
football	fotball(en)	*foowtbal*
football match	fotballkamp(en)	*foowtbalkamp*
goggles	svømmebriller	*svurmebriller*
golf	golf	*'golf*
golf course	golfbane(n)	*golfbahneh*
to go hillwalking	gå tur i fjellet	*gaw toor ee fyelleh*
ice hockey	ishockey	*ees-hockey*
to go jogging	jogge	*yoggeh*
lake	innsjø(en)	*inshur*
racket	racket(en)	*'racket'*
to ride	ri	*ree*
rock climbing	fjellklatring(en)	*fyell-klatring*
to row	ro	*roh*
rowing boat	robåt(en)	*rohbawt*
to run	springe	*spring-eh*
to sail	seile	*sileh*
sailboard	seilbrett(et)	*silbrett*

sand	sand(en)	*sann*
sea	sjø(en)	*shur*
to skate	gå på skøyter	*gaw paw shoyter*
skates	skøyter	*shoyter*
skating rink	skøytebane(n)	*shoyteh-bahneh*
to ski	gå på ski	*gaw paw shee*
skiing (*downhill*)	utforkjøring(en)	*ootforHyurring*
(*slalom*)	slalåmkjøring(en)	*shlahlawm-Hyurring*
(*cross-country*)	langrenn(et)	*langrenn*
skin diving	dykking(en)	*dEWkking*
ski pass	skiheiskort(et)	*shee-hISskort*
skis	ski	*shee*
ski sticks	skistaver	*sheestahver*
ski tow	skiheis(en)	*shee-hISS*
ski wax	skismøring(en)	*sheesmurring*
stadium	stadion	*stahdion*
to swim	svømme	*svurmeh*
swimming pool	svømmebasseng(et)	*svurmebasseng*
tennis	tennis	*tennis*
tennis court	tennisbane(n)	*tennisbahneh*
tennis racket	tennisracket(en)	*tennisracket*
to go walking	gå tur	*gaw toor*
to go water-skiing	stå på vannski	*staw paw vannshee*
water-skis	vannski	*vannshee*
wave	bølge(en)	*burlgeh*
wet suit	våtdrakt(en)	*vawtdrakt*
to go windsurfing	kjøre seilbrett	*Hyurreh sIlbrett*
yacht	seilbåt(en)	*sIlbawt*

How do I get to the beach?
Hvordan kommer jeg til stranden?
vohrdan kommer yI til strannen

How deep is the water here?
Hvor dypt er vannet her?
vohr dEWpt ar vanneh har

Is there an indoor/outdoor pool here?
Er det et innendørs/utendørs svømmebasseng her?
ar deh et innendurrss/ootendurrss svurmebasseng har

Is it safe to swim here?
Er det trygt å bade her?
ar deh trewkt aw bahdeh har

Can I fish here?
Kan jeg fiske her?
kan yi fiskeh har

Do I need a fishing permit?
Trenger jeg fiskekort?
treng-er yi fiskekort

Where can I hire ...?
Hvor kan jeg leie ...?
vohr kan yi li-eh

I would like to hire ...
Jeg vil gjerne leie ...
yi vil yarneh li-eh

How much does it cost per hour/day?
Hvor mye koster det pr. time/dag?
vohr mew-eh koster deh par teemeh/dahg

How much is a weekly pass for the ski lift?
Hvor mye koster et ukekort for skiheisen?
vohr mew-eh koster et ookehkort for shee-hissen

I'd like to try cross-country skiing
Jeg vil gjerne prøve langrenn
yi vil yarneh prurveh langrenn

I would like to take water-skiing lessons
Jeg vil gjerne ha vannski-timer
yı vil yɑrneh hah vɑnnshee-teemer

THINGS YOU'LL SEE

avgrenset område	restricted area
badeområde	bathing area
billetter	tickets
forbudt	forbidden
fotballbane	football pitch
føre	snow conditions for skiing
førstehjelp	first aid
gangsti	footpath
havn	port, harbour
havnepoliti	harbour police
ingen bading	no swimming
ingen fisking	no fishing
ingen stuping	no diving
løype	track
merket løype	marked footpath/ cross-country ski path
rasfare	danger of avalanche
seilbåter	sailing boats
skiheis	ski lift
sportsmuligheter	sporting facilities
sportssenter	sports centre
stadion	stadium
strand	beach
sykkelsti	cycle path
sykler	bicycles
tennisbane	tennis court
til leie	for hire
travbane	racecourse (horses)
vannsport	water sports

POST OFFICES AND BANKS

Post offices can be identified by a red and gold sign with the word 'Post'. Opening hours are usually 8.30 am to 6 pm on weekdays and 9 am to around 1 pm on Saturdays. Stamps can also be bought in many shops selling postcards. Postboxes are red with a picture of a gold bugle.

Most banks are open during the week from 8 am to 3.30 pm (later on Thursdays) and are closed on Saturdays. Foreign currency and traveller's cheques can also be exchanged at some of the larger information centres and hotels.

The Norwegian unit of currency is the **krone** (*krohneh*). One **krone** is divided into 100 øre (*urreh*) and the coins come in 50 øre, 1 **krone**, 5, 10 and 20 **kroner** (*krohner*). Notes are available in 50, 100, 200, 500 and 1,000 **kroner**.

Credit cards **kredittkort** (*kredittkort*) are widely used. It is also possible to withdraw money from an autobank (**minibank**) using credit cards, although in some cases there may be a charge for this type of transaction.

USEFUL WORDS AND PHRASES

airmail	flypost	*flEWpawst*
bank	bank(en)	*bank*
banknote	pengeseddel(en)	*peng-eseddel*
to change	veksle	*veksleh*
cheque	sjekk(en)	*shekk*
collection	tømming(en)	*turming*
counter	skranke(n)	*skrangkeh*
credit card	kredittkort(et)	*kredittkort*
customs form	tolldeklarasjon	*tawldeklarashohn*
delivery	levering(en)	*levayring*
to deposit	sette inn	*setteh in*
exchange rate	valutakurs(en)	*valootakoorss*
fax	fax	*'fax'*
form	skjema(et)	*shayma*

international money order	internasjonal postanvisning(en)	*internashohnal postanveessning*
letter	brev(et)	*brev*
letter box	postkasse(n)	*pawstkasseh*
mail (*noun*)	post(en)	*pawst*
money order	postanvisning(en)	*pawstanveessning*
package/parcel	pakke(n)	*pakkeh*
post	post(en)	*pawst*
postage rates	porto(en)	*pohrtoh*
postcard	postkort(et)	*pawstkort*
postcode	postkode(n)	*pawstkohdeh*
poste restante	poste restante	*pawst restangt*
postman	postbud(en)	*pawstbood*
post office	postkontor(et)	*pawstkohntohr*
pound sterling	pund(et)	*poon*
registered letter	rekommandert brev	*rekommandayrt brev*
stamp	frimerke(t)	*free-markeh*
surface mail	vanlig post	*vanli pawst*
telegram	telegram(met)	*telegram*
traveller's cheque	reisesjekk(en)	*rissehshekk*

How much is a letter/postcard to …?
Hvor mye koster det å sende et brev/kort til …?
vohr mEW-eh koster deh aw senneh et brev/kort til

I would like three 4-kroner stamps
Kan jeg få tre 4-kroners frimerker?
kan yı faw tray feereh krohnerss freemarker

I want to register this letter
Jeg skal sende dette brevet rekommandert
yı skal senneh detteh breveh rekommandayrt

I want to send this parcel to …
Jeg skal sende denne pakken til …
yi skal senneh denneh pakken til

How long does the post to … take?
Hvor lang tid tar posten til …?
vohr lang teed tahr pawsten til

Where can I post this?
Hvor kan jeg poste dette?
vohr kan yi pawsteh detteh

Is there any mail for me?
Er det noe post til meg?
ar deh no-eh pawst til mi

I'd like to send a fax
Jeg skal sende et fax
yi skal senneh et fax

This is to go airmail
Dette skal gå med flypost
detteh skal gaw may flEWpawst

I'd like to change this into kroner
Jeg vil gjerne veksle dette i kroner
yi vil yarneh veksleh detteh ee krohner

Can I cash these traveller's cheques?
Kan jeg få veksle disse reisesjekkene?
kan yi faw veksleh deesseh rissehshekkeneh

What is the exchange rate for the pound?
Hva er kursen for pund?
vah ar koorsen for poon

THINGS YOU'LL SEE

adressat/mottaker	addressee
adresse	address
avgift	fee
avsender	sender
brev	letter
ekspedisjon	service
flypost/luftpost	airmail
frimerke	stamp
fyll ut	fill in
gebyr	charges
innbetaling	deposits
innenriks porto	inland postage
kasse	cashier
minibank	cash point
pakke	parcel
porto	postage
portotakster	postage rates
postanvisning	money order
postkasse	letter box
postkode/postnummer	postcode
postkontor	post office
postkort	postcard
rekommandert brev	registered mail
sted	place
telegrammer	telegrams
til utlandet	abroad
trykksaker	printed matter
tømmes/tømming	collection times
utbetaling	withdrawals
utenlands porto	overseas postage
valuta	foreign currency
valutakurs	exchange rate
veksling	exchange
åpningstider	opening hours

COMMUNICATIONS

Telephones: There are plenty of public telephone boxes and booths all over Norway and a large number have instructions in English. All telephone directories include a guide in English on how to use the telephone.

Public telephones take both 1 krone and 5, 10 and 20 kroner coins which are lined up at the top of the telephone and fall in as they are needed.

The dialling and engaged tones are similar to the UK ones, but the ringing tone is a repeated long tone.

To phone the UK direct, dial 00-44 (00-1 for the US) followed by the number, omitting the first 0 of the area code. The number for directory enquiries for Norway and Scandinavian countries is 180; for international enquiries the number is 181. For connections through the operator dial 117 for Norway and 115 for abroad.

Local emergency numbers for police, fire and ambulance are listed inside the front cover of the telephone directory and displayed in telephone boxes – S.O.S. or **øyeblikkelig hjelp.**

USEFUL WORDS AND PHRASES

ambulance	ambulanse(n)	*amboolangsseh*
answering machine	telefonsvarer(en)	*telefohn-svarehr*
call (*verb*)	ringe	*ring-eh*
(*noun*)	telefonsamtale(n)	*telefohnsamtahleh*
casualty department	legevakt(en)	*layg-eh-vakt*
crossed line	feil på linjen	*fil paw leen-yen*
to dial	slå nummeret	*slaw noommereh*
dialling tone	summetone(n)	*soommetohneh*
directory enquiries	opplysningen	*opplEWssning-en*
engaged	opptatt	*opptat*
enquiries	opplysninger	*opplEWssning-er*
extension	linje(n)	*leen-yeh*
fire brigade	brannvesen(et)	*brannvayssen*

international call	internasjonal samtale	*internashohnal samtahleh*
internet	internett(et)	*internett(eh)*
mobile phone	mobiltelefon(en)	*mohbeel-telefohn(ayn)*
modem	modem(et)	*mohdem(eh)*
number	nummer(et)	*noommer*
payphone	telefon-automat(en)	*telefohn-owtohmaht*
phonecard	telefonkort(et)	*telefohn-kort(eh)*
police	politi	*pohlitee*
receiver	rør(et)	*rurr*
reverse charge call	noteringsover-føring(en)	*nohtayringssawver-furring*
telephone	telefon(en)	*telefohn*
telephone directory	telefonkatalog(en)	*telefohnkatalawg*
Web site	web side(n)	*vebb seedeh(n)*
wrong number	feil nummer	*fil noommer*

Where is the nearest phone box?
Hvor er nærmeste telefonkiosk?
vohr ar narmesteh telefohnнyawsk

I would like the directory for ...
Kan jeg få låne telefonkatalogen for ...?
kan yı faw lawneh telefohnkatalawgen for

Can I call abroad from here?
Kan jeg ringe utlandet herfra?
kan yı ring-eh ootlanneh harfrah

How much is a call to ...?
Hvor mye koster en telefonsamtale til ...?
vohr mɛw-eh koster ayn telefohnsamtahleh til

I would like to reverse the charges
Kan jeg ringe noteringsoverføring?
kan yı ring-eh nohtayringssawverfurring

I would like a number in …
Jeg skal ha et nummer i …
yɪ skal hah et noommer ee

Hello, this is … speaking
Hallo, dette er …
hallo, detteh ar

Is that …?
Er det …?
ar deh

Speaking
Ja, det er meg
yah deh ar mɪ

I would like to speak to …
Kan jeg få snakke med …?
kan yɪ faw snakkeh may

Extension …, please
Kan jeg få linje …?
kan yɪ faw leen-yeh

Please tell him/her … called
Kan du si at … har ringt?
kan doo see at … hahr ringt

Ask him/her to call me back, please
Kan du be ham/henne ringe meg?
kan doo bay ham/henneh ring-eh mɪ

My number is 435-48652
Mitt nummer er fire-tre-fem fire-åtte-seks-fem-to
mit noommer ar feereh-treh fem feereh-awtteh seks fem-toh

Do you know where he/she is?
Vet du hvor han/hun er?
vayt doo vohr han/hoon ar

When will he/she be back?
Når kommer han/hun tilbake?
nawr kommer han/hoon tilbahkeh

Could you leave him/her a message?
Kan du gi ham/henne en beskjed?
kan doo yee ham/henneh ayn beshay

I'll ring back later
Jeg ringer igjen senere
yı ring-er ee-yen saynereh

Sorry, wrong number
Unnskyld, feil nummer
oonshEWl fil noommer

What's your fax number/email address?
Hva er ditt fax nummer/epost adresse?
vah ar ditt faks noommer/ay-pawst adresseh

Can I send an email/fax from here?
Kan jeg sende epost/en fax herfra?
kan yı senneh ay-pawst/ayn faks hayr-frah

Can I use the photocopier/fax machine?
Kan jeg bruke kopimaskinen/faxen?
kan yı brookeh kohpimasheenen/faksen

How do I get an outside line?
Hvordan kan jeg ringe ut?
vohrdann kan yı ring-eh oot

THINGS YOU'LL SEE

feilmelding	faults service
fjerntakst	operator; long-distance calls
fjernvalg	direct dialling
gebyr	fee
innenlands	national
i ustand	out of order
lokalsamtale	local call
retningsnummer	dialling code
takst	charges
utlandet	international

THINGS YOU'LL HEAR

Hvem skal du snakke med?
Who would you like to speak to?

Hvem er det som snakker?
Who's speaking?

Hva er ditt nummer?
What is your number?

Han/hun er dessverre ikke inne
Sorry, he/she is not in

Han/hun kommer tilbake klokken ett
He/she will be back at one o'clock

Kan du ringe igjen i morgen?
Can you call back tomorrow?

Jeg skal si fra at du har ringt
I'll tell him/her you called

HEALTH

If a British subject falls ill in Norway, he or she will have to pay for medical treatment in the same way as Norwegians do: a small standard fee has to be paid for a doctor's appointment and patients have to pay the full price for medicines on prescription. Hospital treatment is free apart from a small standard fee similar to what you pay a GP. Doctors don't usually go out on call after surgery hours. If you require urgent medical treatment go to a hospital casualty department. You will find the telephone numbers for the ambulance service and hospitals inside the front cover of the telephone directory.

The **apotek** or chemist's is open during normal shopping hours. In the evenings, in larger towns, medicines can be obtained from a duty chemist, but elsewhere medicines can be obtained from the doctor on call.

Dental treatment must be paid for in full.

USEFUL WORDS AND PHRASES

abscess	byll(en)	bEwll
accident	ulykke(n)	oolEwkeh
ambulance	ambulanse(n)	amboolangsseh
anaemic	anemisk	anaymisk
appendicitis	blindtarmbetennelse(n)	blinntarmbetennelseh
appendix	blindtarm(en)	blinntarm
aspirin	aspirin(en)	aspireen
asthma	astma(en)	assma
backache	vondt i ryggen	vohnt i rEwggen
bandage	bandasje(n)	bandahsheh
bite		
(by dog/adder)	bitt(et)	bitt
(by insect)	stikk(et)	stikk
bladder	blære(n)	blar-eh
blister	blemme(n)	blemmeh
blood	blod	bloh

blood pressure	blodtrykk(et)	*blohtrEWkk*
burn *(noun)*	brannsår(et)	*brannsawr*
cancer	kreft	*kreft*
casualty department	legevakt(en)	*layg-eh-vakt*
chemist	apotek(et)	*apohtayk*
chest	bryst(et)	*brEWst*
chickenpox	vannkopper	*vannkopper*
cold *(noun)*	forkjølelse(n)	*forHyurlelseh*
concussion	hjernerystelse(n)	*yarnerEWstelseh*
constipation	treg avføring	*trayg ahvfurring*
contact lenses	kontaktlinser	*kohntaktlinsser*
corn	liktorn(en)	*leektohrn*
cough *(noun)*	hoste(n)	*hohsteh*
cut	kutt(et)	*koott*
dentist	tannlege(n)	*tannlaygeh*
diabetes	diabetes	*deeabaytehs*
diarrhoea	diaré(en)	*dee-aray*
dizzy	svimmel	*svimmel*
doctor	lege	*laygeh*
earache	øreverk(en)	*urrevark*
fever	feber(en)	*fayber*
filling	plombe(n)	*plohmbeh*
first aid	førstehjelp(en)	*furrsteh-yelp*
flu	influensa(en)	*influenssa*
fracture	brudd(et)	*broodd*
German measles	røde hunder	*rurdeh hoonner*
glasses	briller	*briller*
haemorrhage	blødning(en)	*blurdning*
hay fever	høysnue(n)	*hoysnoo-eh*
headache	hodepine(n)	*hohdepeeneh*
heart	hjerte(t)	*yarteh*
heart attack	hjerteinfarkt(et)	*yarteh-infarkt*
hospital	sykehus(et)	*sEWkeh-hooss*
ill	syk	*sEWk*
indigestion	dårlig fordøyelse	*dawrli fordoyelseh*
inflammation	betennelse(n)	*betennelseh*

injection	sprøyte(n)	*sproyteh*
itch	kløe(n)	*klur-eh*
kidney	nyre(n)	*nEWreh*
lump	kul(en)	*kool*
measles	meslinger	*messling-er*
migraine	migrene(n)	*meegrayneh*
mumps	kusma	*koossma*
nausea	kvalme(n)	*kvalmeh*
nurse	sykepleier(en)	*sEWkehplI-er*
operation	operasjon(en)	*ohperashohn*
optician	optiker(en)	*optiker*
pain	smerte(n)	*smarteh*
penicillin	penicillin(en)	*penisilleen*
plaster (*sticking*)	plaster(et)	*plaster*
plaster of Paris	gips(en)	*yeeps*
pneumonia	lungebetennelse(n)	*loongehbetennelseh*
pregnant	gravid	*graveed*
prescription	resept(en)	*resept*
rheumatism	revmatisme(n)	*revmatissmeh*
scald (*noun*)	brannsår(et)	*brannsawr*
scratch	skrubbsår(et)	*skroobbsawr*
sore throat	vondt i halsen	*vohnt ee hal-sen*
splinter	flis(en)	*fleess*
to sprain	forstue	*for-stoo-eh*
sting	stikk(et)	*stikk*
stomach	mage(n)	*mahgeh*
temperature	feber(en)	*fayber*
tonsils	mandler	*mandler*
toothache	tannverk(en)	*tannvark*
travel sickness	reisesyke(n)	*rIsseh-sEWkeh*
ulcer	magesår(et)	*mahgesawr*
vaccination	vaksinasjon(en)	*vaksinashohn*
to vomit	kaste opp	*kasteh opp*
whooping cough	kikhoste(n)	*HyeeK-hohsteh*
X-ray	røntgen	*rurnken*

I have a pain in …
Jeg har vondt i …
yı hahr vohnt ee

I do not feel well
Jeg føler meg ikke bra
yı f̱urler mı ı̱kkeh brah

I feel faint
Jeg tror jeg besvimer
yı trohr yı besve̱emer

I feel sick
Jeg er kvalm
yı ar kvalm

I feel dizzy
Jeg er svimmel
yı ar svı̱mmel

It hurts here
Det gjør vondt her
deh yurr vohnt har

It's a sharp pain
Det er en skarp smerte
deh ar ayn skarp sma̱rteh

It hurts all the time
Det gjør vondt hele tiden
deh yurr vohnt ha̱yleh te̱eden

It only hurts now and then
Det gjør bare vondt av og til
deh yurr ba̱hreh vohnt ahv aw til

It hurts when you touch it
Det gjør vondt når du tar på det
deh yurr vohnt nawr doo tahr paw deh

It hurts more at night
Det gjør mere vondt om natten
deh yurr mayreh vohnt om natten

It stings
Det svir
deh sveer

It aches
Det verker
deh varker

I have a temperature
Jeg har feber
yı hahr fayber

I need a prescription for …
Jeg trenger en resept på …
yı treng-er ayn resept paw

I normally take …
Jeg tar vanligvis …
yı tahr vahnliveess

I'm allergic to …
Jeg er allergisk mot …
yı ar allargisk moht

Have you got anything for …?
Har du noe for …?
hahr doo no-eh for

Can you take these if you're pregnant/breastfeeding?
Kan du ta disse hvis du er gravid/ammer?
kan doo tah disseh vees doo ar grahveed/ammer

I'm ... months pregnant
Jeg er gravid i ... måned
yı ar grahveed ee ... mawnet

Do I need a prescription for ...?
Trenger jeg resept på ...?
treng-er yı resept paw

I have lost a filling
Jeg har mistet en plombe
yı hahr mistet ayn plohmbeh

THINGS YOU'LL SEE

ambulanse	ambulance
apotek	chemist
briller	glasses
... ganger daglig	... times a day
i forbindelse med mat/måltid	to be taken at mealtimes
klinikk	clinic
lege	doctor
legekontor	surgery
legevakt	casualty department
medisin	medicine
optiker	optician
resept	prescription
ryst flasken/omrystes	shake the bottle
sykehus	hospital
tannlege	dentist
1 teskje (5 ml)	1 teaspoonful (5 ml)

→

undersøkelse	check-up, examination
utenom mat/måltid	between meals
utvortes bruk	external use
vakthavende apotek	duty chemist
visitt-tid	visiting hours
øyeblikkelig hjelp	emergencies

THINGS YOU'LL HEAR

Ta ... tabletter av gangen
Take ... tablets at a time

Med vann
With water

Kan tygges
May be chewed

En gang/to ganger/tre ganger daglig
Once/twice/three times a day

Bare før sengetid
Only when you go to bed

Det har vi dessverre ikke
I'm sorry, we don't have that

Det må du ha resept på
For that you need a prescription

Jeg tror du skal gå til lege
I think you should see a doctor

CONVERSION TABLES

DISTANCES

Distances are marked in kilometres. To convert kilometres to
miles, divide the km by 8 and multiply by 5 (one km being
five-eights of a mile). Convert miles to km by dividing the
miles by 5 and multiplying by 8. A mile is 1609 m (1.609 km).

km	miles *or* km	miles
1.61	1	0.62
3.22	2	1.24
4.83	3	1.86
6.44	4	2.48
8.05	5	3.11
9.66	6	3.73
11.27	7	4.35
12.88	8	4.97
14.49	9	5.59
16.10	10	6.21

Other units of length:

1 centimetre	= 0.39 in	1 inch	= 25.4 millimetres
1 metre	= 39.37 in	1 foot	= 0.30 metre (30 cm)
10 metres	= 32.81 ft	1 yard	= 0.91 metre

WEIGHTS

The unit you will come into most contact with is the kilogram
(kilo), equivalent to 2 lb 3 oz. To convert kg to lbs, multiply
by 2 and add one-tenth of the result (thus, 6 kg x 2 = 12 + 1.2,
or 13.2 lbs). One ounce is about 28 grams, and 1 lb is 454 g.

grams	ounces	ounces	grams
50	1.76	1	28.3
100	3.53	2	56.7
250	8.81	4	113.4
500	17.63	8	226.8

kg	lbs or kg	lbs
0.45	1	2.20
0.91	2	4.41
1.36	3	6.61
1.81	4	8.82
2.27	5	11.02
2.72	6	13.23
3.17	7	15.43
3.63	8	17.64
4.08	9	19.84
4.53	10	22.04

TEMPERATURE

To convert centigrade or Celsius degrees into Fahrenheit, the accurate method is to multiply the °C figure by 1.8 and add 32. Similarly, to convert °F to °C, subtract 32 from the °F figure and divide by 1.8. This will give you a truly accurate conversion, but takes a little time in mental arithmetic! See the table below.

°C	°F	°C	°F	
-10	14	25	77	
0	32	30	86	
5	41	36.9	98.4	*body temperature*
10	50	40	104	
20	68	100	212	*boiling point*

LIQUIDS

Motorists from the UK will be used to seeing petrol priced per litre (and may even know that one litre is about 1.75 pints). One 'imperial' gallon is roughly 4.5 litres, but American drivers must remember that the US gallon is 3.8 litres (1 litre = 1.06 US quart). In the following table, imperial gallons are used:

litres	gals or l	gals
4.54	1	0.22
9.10	2	0.44
13.64	3	0.66
18.18	4	0.88
22.73	5	1.10
27.27	6	1.32
31.82	7	1.54
36.37	8	1.76
40.91	9	1.98
45.46	10	2.20
90.92	20	4.40
136.38	30	6.60
181.84	40	8.80
227.30	50	11.00

TYRE PRESSURES

lb/sq in	15	18	20	22	24
kg/sq cm	1.1	1.3	1.4	1.5	1.7

lb/sq in	26	28	30	33	35
kg/sq cm	1.8	2.0	2.1	2.3	2.5

MINI-DICTIONARY

about: about 16 cirka 16
accelerator gasspedal(en)
accident ulykke(n)
accommodation overnatting(en)
ache verk(en)
acid rain sur nedbør
adder huggorm(en)
address adresse(n)
adhesive lim(et)
admission charge inngangsbillett(en)
after etter
aftershave etterbarberingsvann(et)
again igjen
against mot
Aids aids
aircraft fly(et)
air freshener luftrenser(en)
air hostess flyvertinne(n)
airline flyselskap(et)
airport flyplass(en)
alarm clock vekkerklokke(n)
alcohol alkohol(en)
all alle
  all the streets alle gatene
  that's all, thanks det er alt, takk
almost nesten
alone alene
already allerede
always alltid
am: I am jeg er
ambulance ambulanse(n)
America Amerika
American *(person)* amerikaner(en)
  (adj) amerikansk
and og
ankle ankel(en)
anorak anorak(en)
another *(different)* en annen

another: *(one more)* en til
  another room et annet rom
  another coffee, please
  en kaffe til, takk
answering machine telefonsvarer(en)
antifreeze frysevæske(n)
antique shop antikvitetshandel(en)
antiseptic antiseptisk
apartment leilighet(en)
aperitif aperitiff(en)
appetite appetitt(en)
apple eple(t)
application form søknadsskjema(et)
appointment *(business)* avtale(n)
  (at hairdresser's etc) time(n)
apricot aprikos(en)
Arctic Circle polarsirkel(en)
Arctic Ocean Nordishavet
are: you/we/they are du/vi/de er
arm arm(en)
art kunst(en)
art gallery kunstgalleri(et)
artist kunstner(en)
as: as soon as possible
  så snart som mulig
ashtray askebeger(et)
asleep: he's asleep han sover
aspirin aspirin(en)
at: at the post office på
  postkontoret
  at night om natten
  at 3 o'clock klokken tre
attractive pen
aunt tante(n)
Australia Australia
Australian *(person)* australier(en)
  (adj) australsk
Austria østerrike

Austrian *(person)* østerriker(en)
  (adj) østerriksk
automatic automatisk
away: is it far away?
  er det langt borte?
  go away! forsvinn!
awful fryktelig
axle aksel(en)

baby baby(en)
baby wipes våtserviett(en) for barn
back *(not front)* bak
  (body) rygg(en)
  I'll come back tomorrow
  jeg kommer tilbake i morgen
bacon bacon(et)
  bacon and eggs egg og bacon
bad dårlig
bait agn(et)
bake bake
baker baker(en)
balcony balkong(en)
ball ball(en)
ball-point pen kulepenn(en)
banana banan(en)
band *(musicians)* band(et)
bandage bandasje(n)
bank bank(en)
banknote pengeseddel(en)
bar *(drinks)* bar(en)
  bar of chocolate
  sjokoladeplate(n)
barbecue grill(en)
barber's herrefrisør(en)
Barents Sea Barentshavet
bargain (et) godt kjøp
basement kjeller(en)
basin *(sink)* vask(en)
basket kurv(en)
bath bad(et)
  (tub) badekar(et)
  to have a bath bade

bathroom bad(et)
battery batteri(et)
beach strand(en)
beans bønner
beard skjegg(et)
because fordi
bed seng(en)
bed linen sengetøy(et)
bedroom soverom(met)
beef oksekjøtt(et)
beer øl(et)
before ... før ...
beginner nybegynner(en)
behind ... bak ...
beige beige
Belgian *(person)* belgier(en)
  (adj) belgisk
Belgium Belgia
bell klokke(n)
  (door) dørklokke(n)
below ... under ...
belt belte(t)
beside ved siden av
best best
better bedre
between ... mellom ...
bicycle sykkel(en)
big stor
bikini bikini(en)
bill regning(en)
bin liner søppelpose(n)
bird fugl(en)
birthday fødselsdag(en)
  happy birthday!
  gratulerer med dagen!
birthday present
  fødselsdagspresang(en)
biscuit kjeks(en)
bite *(noun: by dog, adder)* bitt(et)
  (by insect) stikk(et)
  (verb) bite
bitter bitter
black sort, svart

blackberries bjørnebær
blanket ullteppe(t)
bleach *(noun)* blekemiddel(et)
　(verb: hair) bleke
blind *(cannot see)* blind
　(window) rullegardin(en)
blister blemme(n)
blizzard snøstorm(en)
blood blod(et)
blouse bluse(n)
blue blå
blueberries blåbær
boat båt(en)
body kropp(en)
boil *(verb)* koke
bolt *(noun: on door)* bolt(en)
　(verb) bolte
bone ben(et)
bonnet *(car)* panser(et)
book *(noun)* bok(en)
　(verb) bestille
booking office billettkontor(et)
bookshop bokhandel(en)
boot *(car)* bagasjerom(met)
　(footwear) støvel(en)
border grense(n)
boring kjedelig
born: I was born in ...
　jeg er født i ...
both begge
　both of them/us begge to
　both ... and ... både ... og ...
bottle flaske(n)
bottle opener flaskeåpner(en)
bottom bunn(en)
　(part of body) bak(en)
　(of sea) havbunn(en)
bowl bolle(n)
box eske(n)
boy gutt(en)
boyfriend kjæreste(n)
bra behå(en)
bracelet armbånd(et)

braces seler
brake *(noun)* brems(en)
　(verb) bremse
brandy konjakk(en)
bread brød(et)
breakdown *(car)* havari(et)
　(nervous) nervesammenbrudd(et)
　I've had a breakdown
　(car) jeg har fått motorstopp
breakfast frokost(en)
breathe puste
　I can't breathe jeg får ikke puste
bridge bro(en)
　(game) bridge
briefcase dokumentmappe(n)
British britisk
brochure brosjyre(n)
broken i stykker
　broken leg brukket ben
brooch nål(en)
brother bror(en)
brown brun
bruise blått merke, blåmerke
brush *(noun)* børste(n)
　(paint) pensel(en)
　(sweeping) sopekost(en)
　(verb: hair, teeth) børste
　(verb: floor) sope
bucket bøtte(n)
building bygning(en)
bumper støtfanger(en)
burglar innbruddstyv(en)
burn *(noun)* brannsår(et)
　(verb) brenne
bus buss(en)
business forretning(en)
　it's none of your business
　det angår ikke deg
bus station buss-stasjon(en)
busy *(occupied)* opptatt
　(street) travel
but men
butcher slakter(en)

butter smør(et)
button knapp(en)
buy kjøpe
by: by the window ved vinduet
  by Friday innen fredag
  by myself alene

cabbage kål(en)
cable car taubane(n)
cable TV kabel TV(en)
café kafé(en)
cagoule regnjakke(n)
cake kake(n)
calculator kalkulator(en)
call: what's it called? hva heter det?
camcorder videokamera(et)
camera kamera(et)
campsite campingplass(en)
camshaft kamaksel(en)
can (tin) boks(en)
can: can I have ...? kan jeg få ...?
Canada Canada
Canadian (person) kanadier(en)
  (adj) kanadisk
cancer kreft(en)
candle stearinlys(et)
canoe kano(en)
cap (bottle) kork(en)
  (hat) lue(n)
car bil(en)
caravan campingvogn(en)
carburettor forgasser(en)
card kort(et)
cardigan golfjakke(n)
careful forsiktig
  be careful! vær forsiktig!
carpet gulvteppe(t)
carriage (train) vogn(en)
carrot gulrot(en)
carrycot bærebag(en)
car seat (for a baby) barnesete(t)
case (suitcase) koffert(en)

cash (money) kontanter
  (verb) løse inn
  to pay cash betale kontant
cash point minibank(en)
cassette kassett(en)
cassette player kassettspiller(en)
castle slott(et)
cat katt(en)
cathedral katedral(en)
cauliflower blomkål(en)
cave hule(n)
cemetery kirkegård(en)
centre (shopping, sports) senter(et)
  (of city) sentrum
certificate bevis(et)
chair stol(en)
chambermaid værelsespike(n)
chamber music
  kammermusikk(en)
change (noun: money) vekslepenger
  (verb: clothes) skifte
cheap billig
cheers! skål!
cheese ost(en)
chemist (shop) apotek(et)
cheque sjekk(en)
chequebook sjekkhefte(t)
cherry kirsebær(et)
chess sjakk
chest (part of body) bryst(et)
chest of drawers kommode(n)
chewing gum tyggegummi(en)
chicken kylling(en)
child barn(et)
  children barn
china porselen(et)
China Kina
Chinese (person) kineser(en)
  (adj) kinesisk
chips pommes frites
chocolate sjokolade(n)
  box of chocolates
  (en) eske konfekt

chop *(food)* kotelett(en)
  (to cut) hakke
Christian name fornavn(et)
church kirke(n)
  church service gudstjeneste(n)
cigar sigar(en)
cigarette sigarett(en)
cinema kino(en)
city by(en)
city centre sentrum
class klasse(n)
classical music klassisk musikk
clean *(adj)* ren
clear klar
  is that clear? er det klart?
clever flink
clock klokke(n)
close *(near)* nær
  (stuffy) dårlig luft
close *(verb)* lukke
  the shop is closed
  forretningen er lukket/stengt
clothes klær
cloudberries multer
club klubb(en)
  (cards) kløver
clutch clutch(en)
coach turbuss(en)
  (of train) vogn(en)
coach station buss-stasjon(en)
coat *(men)* frakk(en)
  (women) kåpe(n)
coat hanger kleshenger(en)
coffee kaffe(n)
coin mynt(en)
cold *(illness)* forkjølelse(n)
  (adj) kald
  I have a cold jeg er forkjølet
  I am cold jeg fryser
  it's cold det er kaldt
cold buffet koldtbord(et)
collar krave(n)
  (on shirts) snipp(en)

collection *(stamps etc)* samling(en)
colour farge(n)
colour film fargefilm(en)
comb *(noun)* kam(men)
  (verb) gre
come komme
  I come from …
  jeg kommer fra …
  we came last week
  vi kom i forrige uke
  come here! kom hit!
compartment kupé(en)
complicated komplisert
computer datamaskin(en)
concert konsert(en)
conditioner *(hair)* hårbalsam(en)
condom kondom(et)
conductor *(bus)* konduktør(en)
  (orchestra) dirigent(en)
congratulations! gratulerer!
constipation treg avføring
consulate konsulat(et)
contact lenses kontaktlinser
contraceptives preventiver
cook *(noun)* kokk(en)
  (verb) lage mat
cooker komfyr(en)
cooking utensils
  utstyr til matlaging
cool kjølig
cork kork(en)
corkscrew korketrekker(en)
corner hjørne(t)
corridor korridor(en)
cosmetics kosmetikk(en)
cost *(verb)* koste
  what does it cost?
  hva koster det?
cotton bomull(en)
cotton wool bomull(en)
cough *(noun)* hoste(n)
  (verb) hoste
country land(et)

cousin *(male)* fetter(en)
  (female) kusine(n)
crab krabbe(n)
cramp krampe(n)
crayfish kreps(en)
cream krem(en)
credit card kredittkort(et)
crew mannskap(et)
crisps chips
crowded folksom
crown(s) *(unit of currency)* krone(r)
cruise cruise(t)
crutches krykker
cry *(weep)* gråte
  (shout) rope
cucumber slangeagurk(en)
cuff links mansjettknapper
cup kopp(en)
cupboard skap(et)
curls krøller
curry karri(en)
curtain gardin(en)
customs toll(en)
cut *(noun)* kutt(et)
  (verb: with knife) skjære
  (with scissors) klippe

dad pappa(en)
dairy *(shop)* meieri(et)
damp fuktig
dance *(noun)* dans(en)
  (verb) danse
Dane danske(n)
dangerous farlig
Danish dansk
dark mørk
daughter datter(en)
day dag(en)
dead død
deaf døv
dear *(person)* kjær
  (expensive) dyr

deck chair fluktstol(en)
deep dyp
deliberately med hensikt
Denmark Danmark
dentist tannlege(n)
dentures tannprotese(n)
deny nekte
deodorant deodorant(en)
department store varemagasin(et)
departure avgang(en)
develop *(film)* fremkalle
diamond *(jewel)* diamant(en)
  (cards) ruter
diarrhoea diaré(en)
diary dagbok(en)
dictionary ordbok(en)
die dø
diesel diesel(en)
different annerledes
  that's different!
  det er en annen sak!
  I'd like a different one
  kan jeg få en annen?
difficult vanskelig
dining car spisevogn(en)
dining room spisestue(n)
directory *(telephone)* katalog(en)
dirty skitten
disabled funksjonshemmet
disposable nappies engangsbleie(n)
distributor *(car)* fordeler(en)
dive stupe
diving board stupebrett(et)
divorced skilt
do gjøre
doctor lege(n)
document dokument(et)
dog hund(en)
doll dukke(n)
dollar dollar(en)
door dør(en)
double room dobbeltrom(met)
doughnut smultring(en)

down ned
drawing pin tegnestift(en)
dress kjole(n)
drink *(noun: non-alcoholic)* drikk(en)
  (noun: alcoholic) drink(en)
  (verb) drikke
  can I have something to drink?
  kan jeg få noe å drikke?
drinking water drikkevann(et)
drive *(verb)* kjøre
driver sjåfør(en)
driving licence førerkort(et)
drunk full
dry tørr
dry cleaner renseri(et)
dummy *(for baby)* narresmokk(en)
during i løpet av
dustbin søppelkasse(en)
duster støvklut(en)
Dutch *(adj)* hollandsk
Dutchman, Dutchwoman
  hollender(en)
duty-free tollfri
duvet dyne(n)

each *(every)* hver
  twenty kroner each
  tjue kroner hver
early tidlig
earrings øredobber
ears ører
east øst
easy lett
eat spise
egg egg(et)
either: either of them will do
  det er det samme
  either ... or ... enten ... eller ...
elastic elastisk
elastic band strikk(et)
elbow albue(n)
electric elektrisk

electricity elektrisitet
else: something else noe annet
  someone else noen annen
  somewhere else et annet sted
email epost(en)
email address e-mail adresse(n)
embarrassing flaut
embassy ambassade(n)
embroidery broderi(et)
emergency nødssituasjon(en)
emergency brake
  (train) nødbrems(en)
emergency exit nødutgang(en)
empty tom
enamel emalje(n)
end slutt(en)
engaged *(couple)* forlovet
  (occupied) opptatt
engine *(motor)* motor(en)
England England
English engelsk
  she is English hun er engelsk
English Channel den engelske kanal
Englishman engelskmann(en)
Englishwoman engelsk dame
enlargement *(photo)* forstørrelse(n)
enough nok
entertainment underholdning(en)
entrance inngang(en)
envelope konvolutt(en)
escalator rulletrapp(en)
especially spesielt
evening kveld(en)
every hver
everyone alle
everything alt
everywhere overalt
example eksempel(et)
  for example for eksempel
excellent meget bra
excess baggage overvektig bagasje
exchange *(verb)* veksle
exchange rate valutakurs(en)

excursion tur(en)

excuse me!

   (to get attention) unnskyld!

exit utgang(en)

expensive dyr

extension *(on a house)* tilbygg(et)

eye øye(t)

   eyes øyne

eye drops øyendråper

face ansikt(et)

faint *(unclear)* svak

   (verb) besvime

   I feel faint jeg holder på å besvime

fair *(funfair)* tivoli(et)

   (just) **it's not fair** det er urettferdig

false teeth tannprotese(en)

family familie(n)

fan *(ventilator)* vifte(n)

   (enthusiast) finne(n)

fan belt vifterem(en)

fantastic fantastisk

far langt

   how far is it to …?

   hvor langt er det til …?

fare billett(en)

farm bondegård(en)

farmer bonde(n)

fashion mote(n)

fast fort

fat *(person)* fyldig, fet

   (on meat etc) fett

father far(en)

fax telefax(en)

fax machine fax(en)

feel *(touch)* føle

   I feel hot jeg er varm

   I feel like … jeg har lyst på …

   I don't feel well

   jeg føler meg ikke bra

feet føtter

felt-tip pen tusjpenn(en)

fence gjerde(t)

ferry ferge(n)

fever feber(en)

fiancé, fiancée forlovede(n)

field jorde(t)

fig fiken(en)

filling *(in tooth)* plombe(n)

   (in sandwich) pålegg(et)

   (in cake etc) fyll(et)

film film(en)

filter filter(et)

finger finger(en)

Finland Finnland

Finn finne(n)

Finnish finsk

fire bål(et)

   (blaze) brann(en)

fire extinguisher

   brannslukningsapparat(et)

firework fyrverkeri(et)

first først

first aid førstehjelp(en)

first floor annen etasje

fish *(noun)* fisk(en)

fishing: to go fishing dra på fisketur

fishing rod fiskestang(en)

fishmonger fiskebutikk(en)

fizzy brusende

fjord fjord(en)

flag flagg(et)

flash *(camera)* blitz(en)

flat *(level)* flat

   (apartment) leilighet(en)

flavour smak(en)

flea loppe(n)

flight fly(et)

   when is the next flight to …?

   når går neste fly til …?

   we had a pleasant flight

   vi hadde en fin flytur

flippers svømmeføtter

flour mel(et)

flower blomst(en)

flu influensa(en)
flute fløyte(n)
fly *(insect)* flue(n)
   (verb) fly
fog tåke(n)
folk museum folkemuseum
   (folkemuseet)
folk music folkemusikk(en)
food mat(en)
food poisoning matforgiftning(en)
foot fot(en)
football *(game, ball)* fotball(en)
for for
   for me for meg
   what for? for hva?
   for a week for en uke
foreigner utlending(en)
forest skog(en)
fork gaffel(en)
fortnight fjorten dager
fountain pen fyllepenn(en)
fourth fjerde
fracture brudd(et)
France Frankrike
free *(not engaged)* ledig
   (no cost) gratis
freezer fryser(en)
French fransk
   she is French hun er fransk
Frenchman franskmann(en)
Frenchwoman fransk dame
fridge kjøleskap(et)
friend venn(en)
friendly hyggelig
front: in front of … foran …
frost rim(et)
fruit frukt(en)
fruit juice fruktjuice(n)
fry steke
frying pan stekepanne(n)
full full
   I'm full up jeg er forsynt
full board full pensjon

funnel *(for pouring)* trakt(en)
funny morsom
   (odd) rar
furniture møbler

garage garasje(n)
garden hage(n)
garlic hvitløk(en)
gas-permeable contact lenses
   gass-permeable linser
gay *(homosexual)* homoseksuell
gear gir(et)
gear lever girstang(en)
German *(person)* tysker(en)
   (adj) tysk
Germany Tyskland
get *(fetch)* hente
   have you got …? har du …?
   to get the train ta toget
get back: we get back tomorrow
   vi kommer tilbake i morgen
get: to get something back
   få noe igjen
get in *(arrive)* komme til
get off gå av
get on gå på
get out gå ut
get up *(rise)* stå opp
gift gave(n)
gin gin(en)
girl jente (jenta)
girlfriend kjæreste(n)
give gi
glacier isbre(en)
glad glad
glass glass(et)
glasses briller
gloss prints blanke bilder
gloves hansker
glue lim(et)
go gå
   (travel) reise

goggles svømmebriller
gold gull(et)
good god
  good! fint!
goodbye morn'a
government regjering(en)
granddaughter barnebarn(et)
grandfather bestefar(en)
grandmother bestemor(en)
grandson barnebarn(et)
grapes druer
grass gress(et)
Great Britain Storbritannia
green grønn
grey grå
grill grill(en)
grocer (shop) dagligvareforretning(en)
ground floor første etasje
groundsheet teltunderlag(et)
guarantee (noun) garanti(en)
  (verb) garantere
guard vakt(en)
guide book guidebok(en)
guitar gitar(en)
gun (rifle) gevær(et)
  (pistol) pistol(en)

hair hår(et)
hairdresser frisør(en)
hairdryer hårtørrer(en)
hairspray hårlakk(en)
hairstyle hårfasong(en)
half halv
  half an hour en halv time
half board halv pensjon
ham skinke(n)
hamburger hamburger(en)
hammer hammer(en)
hand hånd(en)
handbag håndveske(n)
handbrake håndbrems(en)
handkerchief lommetørkle(t)

handle (door) håndtak(et)
handsome pen
hangover tømmermenn
happy fornøyd
harbour havn(en)
hard hard
  (difficult) vanskelig
hard (contact) lenses harde linser
hat hatt(en)
have ha
  I don't have ... jeg har ikke ...
  can I have ...? kan jeg få ...?
  have you got ...? har du ...?
  I have to go now jeg må gå nå
hay fever høysnue(n)
he han
head hode(t)
headache hodepine(n)
headlights frontlys
hear høre
hearing aid høreapparat(et)
heart hjerte(t)
heart attack hjerteinfarkt(et)
hearts (cards) hjerter
heating oppvarming(en)
heavy tung
heel hæl(en)
hello hallo
help (noun) hjelp(en)
  (verb) hjelpe
  help! hjelp!
hepatitis hepatitt(en)
her: **it's her** det er henne
  it's for her det er til henne
  give it to her gi
  det til henne
  her book/shoes
  hennes bok/sko
  it's hers det er hennes
herring sild(en)
high høy
highway code trafikkreglene
hill bakke(n)

113

him: it's him det er ham
  it's for him det et til ham
  give it to him gi det til ham
hire leie
his: his house/shoes
  hans hus/sko
  it's his det er hans
history historie
hitchhike haike
HIV positive hiv positiv
hobby hobby(en)
holiday ferie(n)
Holland Holland
home: at home hjemme
homeopathy homeopati(en)
honest ærlig
honey honning(en)
honeymoon bryllupsreise(n)
horn horn(et)
horrible fryktelig
hospital sykehus(et)
hot-water bottle varmeflaske(n)
hour time(n)
house hus(et)
how? hvordan?
hungry: I'm hungry jeg er sulten
hurry: I'm in a hurry
  jeg har det travelt
husband mann(en)

I jeg
ice is(en)
ice cream iskrem(en)
ice cube isterning(en)
Iceland Island
Icelander islending(en)
Icelandic islandsk
ice lolly ispinne(n)
ice skates skøyter
ice-skating: to go ice-skating
  gå på skøyter
if hvis

ignition tenning(en)
ill syk
immediately øyeblikkelig
impossible umulig
in i
  in Oslo i Oslo
  in English på engelsk
  in the hotel på hotellet
India India
Indian *(person)* inder(en)
  (adj) indisk
indicator retningsviser(en)
indigestion dårlig fordøyelse
infection infeksjon(en)
information informasjon(en)
inhaler *(for asthma etc)* innhalerer(en)
injection sprøyte(n)
injury skade(n)
ink blekk(et)
inner tube slange(n)
insect insekt(en)
insect repellent myggolje(n)
insomnia søvnløshet(en)
insurance forsikring(en)
interesting interessant
internet internett(et)
interpret tolke
invitation invitasjon(en)
Ireland Irland
Irish irsk
Irishman, Irishwoman irlender(en)
iron *(metal)* jern(et)
  (verb. clothes) stryke
ironmonger jernvarehandel(en)
is: he/she/it is han/hun/det er
island øy(a)
it det
itch *(noun)* kløe(n)
  it itches det klør

jacket jakke(n)
jacuzzi boblebad(et)

jam syltetøy(et)
jazz jazz
jealous sjalu
jeans dongeribukse(n)
jellyfish manet(en)
jeweller gullsmed(en)
job jobb(en)
jog *(verb)* jogge
  to go for a jog
  gå ut og jogge
joke spøk(en)
journey reise(n)
jumper genser(en)
just: it's just arrived
  den har nettopp kommet
  I've just one left
  jeg har bare en igjen

key nøkkel(en)
kidney nyre(n)
kilo kilo(en)
kilometre kilometer(en)
kitchen kjøkken(et)
knee kne(et)
knife kniv(en)
knit strikke
knitwear strikkevarer
know: I don't know jeg vet ikke

label merkelapp(en)
lace blonde(n)
laces *(of shoe)* skolisser
lady dame(n)
lake innsjø(en)
lamb lam(met)
lamp lampe(n)
lampshade lampeskjerm(en)
land *(noun)* land(et)
  (verb) lande
language språk(et)
Lapp same(n)

large stor
last *(final)* siste
  last week i forrige uke
  last month forrige måned
  at last! endelig!
late: it's getting late
  det begynner å bli sent
  the bus is late
  bussen er forsinket
later senere
laugh *(verb)* le
launderette myntvaskeri(et)
laundry *(place)* vaskeri(et)
  (dirty clothes) skittentøy(et)
laxative avføringsmiddel(et)
lazy doven
leaf blad(et)
leaflet brosjyre(n)
learn lære
leather lær(et)
left *(not right)* venstre
  there's nothing left
  det er ikke noe igjen
left luggage locker
  oppbevaringsboks for bagasje
leg ben(et)
lemon sitron(en)
lemonade sitronbrus(en)
length lengde(n)
lens linse(n)
less mindre
lesson undervisningstime(n)
letter brev(et)
letter box postkasse(n)
lettuce salat(en)
library bibliotek(et)
licence sertifikat(et)
life liv(et)
lift *(in building)* heis(en)
  could you give me a lift?
  kan jeg få sitte på?
light *(not heavy)* lett
  (not dark) lys

115

light bulb lyspære(n)
lighter lighter(en)
lighter fuel lighterbensin(en)
light meter lysmåler(en)
like: I like you jeg liker deg
  I like swimming
  jeg liker å svømme
  it's like ... det likner ...
  like this one som denne
lip salve leppepomade(n)
lipstick leppestift(en)
liqueur likør(en)
list liste(n)
litre liter(en)
litter søppel(et)
little (*small*) liten
  it's a little big den er litt stor
  just a little bare litt
liver lever(en)
lollipop kjærlighet på pinne
long lang
  how long does it take?
  hvor lang tid tar det?
lorry lastebil(en)
lost property hittegods(et)
lot: a lot mye
loud (*noise*) høy
lounge stue(n)
love (*noun*) kjærlighet(en)
  (*verb*) elske
lover (*man*) elsker(en)
  (*woman*) elskerinne(n)
low lav
luck hell(et)
  good luck! lykke til!
luggage bagasje(n)
luggage rack bagasjehylle(n)
lunch lunsj(en)
Lutheran luthersk

magazine blad(et)
mail post(en)

make lage
make-up sminke(n)
man mann(en)
manager sjef(en)
map kart(et)
  a map of Oslo et kart over Oslo
marble marmor(en)
market marked(et)
marmalade marmelade(n)
married gift
mascara mascara(en)
mass (*church*) messe(n)
mast mast(en)
match (*light*) fyrstikk(en)
  (*sport*) kamp(en)
material (*cloth*) stoff(et)
mattress madrass(en)
maybe kanskje
me: it's me det er meg
  it's for me det er til meg
  give it to me gi den til meg
meal måltid(et)
meat kjøtt(et)
mechanic mekaniker(en)
medicine medisin(en)
meeting møte(t)
melon melon(en)
men (*toilet*) herretoalett(et)
menu meny(en)
message beskjed(en)
midday klokken tolv
middle: in the middle i midten
midnight midnatt
Midnight Sun midnattssol(en)
milk melk(en), mjølk(a)
mine: it's mine den er min
mineral water mineralvann(et)
minute minutt(en)
mirror speil(et)
Miss frøken
mistake feil(en)
  to make a mistake gjøre en feil
mobile phone mobiltelefon(en)

modem modem(et)
monastery kloster(et)
money penger
month måned(en)
monument monument(et)
moon måne(n)
moped moped(en)
more mer
morning morgen(en)
  in the morning om morgenen
mosaic mosaikk(en)
mosquito mygg(en)
mother mor(en)
motorbike motorsykkel(en)
motorboat motorbåt(en)
motorway motorvei(en)
mountain fjell(et)
mouse mus(en)
moustache bart(en)
mouth munn(en)
move *(verb)* bevege
  (house) flytte
  don't move! ikke rør deg!
movie film(en)
Mr herr
Mrs fru
much: not much ikke mye
  much better/slower
  mye bedre/saktere
mug krus(et)
  a mug of coffee et krus kaffe
mum mamma(en)
museum museum (museet)
mushroom sopp(en)
music musikk(en)
musical instrument
  musikkinstrument(et)
musician musiker(en)
mustard sennep(en)
my: my book min bok
  my house mitt hus
  my keys mine nøkler
mythology mytologi(en)

nail *(metal)* spiker(en)
  (finger) negl(en)
nailfile neglfil(en)
nail polish neglelakk(en)
name navn(et)
  what's your name? hva heter du?
nappy bleie(n)
narrow smal
near: near the door nær døren
  near London
  i nærheten av London
necessary nødvendig
necklace halskjede(t)
need *(verb)* trenge
  I need ... jeg trenger ...
  there's no need
  det er ikke nødvendig
needle nål(en)
negative *(photo)* negativ(et)
neither: neither of them
  ingen av dem
  neither ... nor ...
  hverken ... eller ...
nephew nevø(en)
never aldri
new ny
news nyheter
newsagent bladkiosk(en)
newspaper avis(en)
New Zealand New Zealand
New Zealander newzealender
next neste
  next week neste uke
  next month neste måned
  what next? hva nå?
nice *(attractive)* pen
  (pleasant) hyggelig
  (to eat) god
niece niese(n)
night natt(en)
nightclub nattklubb(en)
nightdress nattkjole(n)
night porter nattevakt(en)

no *(response)* nei
  I have no money
  jeg har ingen penger
noisy bråkete
none ingen
north nord
North Cape Nordkapp
Northern Ireland Nord-Irland
North Pole Nordpol(en)
North Sea Nordsjøen
Norway Norge
Norwegian *(person)* nordmann(en)
  (adj, language) norsk
Norwegian Sea Norskehavet
nose nese(n)
not ikke
notebook notisbok(en)
nothing ingenting
novel roman(en)
now nå
nowhere ingen steder
nudist nudist(en)
number nummer(et)
number plate nummerskilt(et)
nurse sykepleier(en)
nut *(fruit)* nøtt(en)
  (for bolt) mutter(en)

occasionally av og til
of av
office kontor(et)
often ofte
oil olje(n)
ointment salve(n)
OK OK
old gammel
olive oliven(en)
omelette omelett(en)
on ... på ...
one en
onion løk(en)
only bare

open *(verb)* åpne
  (adj) åpen
open sandwich smørbrød(et)
opposite: opposite the hotel
  rett overfor hotellet
optician optiker(en)
or eller
orange *(colour)* oransje
  (fruit) appelsin(en)
orange juice appelsinjuice(n)
orchestra orkester(et)
ordinary *(normal)* vanlig
organ organ(et)
  (music) orgel(et)
our vår
  it's ours den er vår
out: he's out han er ute
outside ute
over ... over ...
  over there der borte
overtake kjøre forbi
oyster østers(en)

pack: pack of cards kortstokk(en)
package pakke(n)
packet pakke(n)
  a packet of ... en pakke ...
padlock hengelås(en)
page side(n)
pain smerte(n)
paint *(noun)* maling(en)
pair par(et)
Pakistan Pakistan
Pakistani *(person)* pakistaner(en)
  (adj) pakistansk
pale blek
pancakes pannekaker
paper papir(et)
paracetamol paracetamol
parcel pakke(n)
pardon? hva?
parents foreldre

park *(noun)* park(en)
  (verb) parkere
parsley persille(n)
party
  (celebration, group) selskap(et)
  (political) parti(et)
passenger passasjer(en)
passport pass(et)
path sti(en)
pavement fortau(et)
pay betale
peach fersken(en)
peanuts peanøtter
pear pære(n)
pearl perle(n)
peas erter
pedestrian fotgjenger(en)
peg *(clothes)* klesklype(n)
  (tent) plugg(en)
pen penn(en)
pencil blyant(en)
pencil sharpener
  blyantspisser(en)
penfriend brevvenn(en)
peninsula halvøy(en)
penknife lommekniv(en)
people folk(et)
pepper pepper(en)
  (red, green) paprika(en)
peppermint peppermynte
per: per night pr. natt
perfect perfekt
perfume parfyme(n)
perhaps kanskje
perm permanent(en)
personal stereo walkman(en)
petrol bensin(en)
petrol station bensinstasjon(en)
phonecard telefonkort(et)
photocopier (foto)kopimaskin(en)
photograph *(noun)* fotografi(et)
  (verb) fotografere
photographer fotograf(en)

phrase book parlør(en)
piano piano(et)
pickpocket lommetyv(en)
picnic picnic(en)
piece stykke(t)
pillow pute(n)
pilot *(air)* flykaptein(en)
pin knappenål(en)
pine *(tree)* furu(en)
pineapple ananas(en)
pink rosa
pipe *(for smoking)* pipe(n)
  (for water) rør(et)
piston stempel(et)
pizza pizza(en)
place sted(et)
  at your place hos deg
plant plante(n)
plaster *(for cut)* plaster(et)
plastic plast(en)
plastic bag plastpose(n)
plate tallerken(en)
platform plattform(en)
play *(theatre)* skuespill(et)
please *(offering)* vær så god
  a cup of coffee, please
  en kopp kaffe, takk
plug *(electrical)* støpsel(et)
  (sink) propp(en)
pocket lomme(n)
poison gift(en)
police politi(et)
police officer politimann(en)
police station politistasjon(en)
politics politikk(en)
poor fattig
  (bad quality) dårlig
pop music popmusikk(en)
pork svinekjøtt(et)
port *(harbour)* havn(en)
porter *(for luggage)* bærer(en)
  (hotel) portier(en)
possible mulig

post (*noun*) post(en)
  (*verb*) poste
postbox postkasse(n)
postcard postkort(et)
poster plakat(en)
postman postbud(et)
post office postkontor(et)
potato potet(en)
poultry høns
pound pund(et)
powder (*cosmetics*) pudder(et)
  (*food*) pulver(et)
pram barnevogn(en)
prawn reke(n)
prescription resept(en)
pretty (*beautiful*) pen
  (*quite*) ganske
priest prest(en)
private privat
problem problem(et)
  what's the problem?
  hva er problemet?
public offentlig
pull trekke
puncture: to have a puncture
  punktere
purple lilla
purse pung(en)
push skyve
pushchair sportsvogn(en)
pyjamas pyjamas(en)

quality kvalitet(en)
quay kai(en)
question spørsmål(et)
queue (*noun*) kø(en)
  (*verb*) stå i kø
quick rask
quiet stille
quite (*fairly*) ganske
  (*fully*) helt

radiator radiator(en)
radio radio(en)
radish reddik(en)
railway line jernbanelinje(n)
rain regn(en)
raincoat regnfrakk(en)
raisins rosiner
rare (*uncommon*) sjelden
  (*steak*) rå
rat rotte(n)
razor blades barberblader
read lese
reading lamp leselampe(n)
  (*bed*) nattbordlampe(n)
ready klar
rear lights baklys
receipt kvittering(en)
receptionist resepsjonist(en)
record (*music*) plate(n)
  (*sporting etc*) rekord(en)
record player platespiller(en)
record shop musikkforretning(en)
red rød
refreshments forfriskninger
registered letter rekommandert brev
reindeer reinsdyr(et)
relative slektning(en)
relax slappe av
religion religion(en)
remember huske
  I don't remember jeg husker ikke
rent (*verb*) leie
reservation reservasjon(en)
rest (*noun: remainder*) rest(en)
  (*verb: relax*) hvile
restaurant restaurant(en)
return (*come back*) komme tilbake
  (*give back*) gi tilbake
return ticket returbillett(en)
rice ris(en)
rich rik
right (*correct*) riktig
  (*direction*) høyre

ring *(to call)* ringe
  (wedding etc) ring(en)
ripe moden
river elv(en)
road vei(en)
rock *(stone)* fjell(et)
  (music) rock
roll *(bread)* rundstykke(t)
roof tak(et)
room rom(met)
  (space) plass(en)
rope tau(et)
rose rose(n)
round *(circular)* rund
  it's my round
  det er min runde
rowing boat robåt(en)
rubber *(eraser)* viskelær(et)
  (material) gummi(en)
rubbish søppel(et)
rucksack ryggsekk(en)
rug *(mat)* matte(n)
  (blanket) pledd(et)
ruin ruin(en)
ruler *(for drawing)* linjal(en)
rum rom(men)
run *(verb)* løpe
runway rullebane(n)
Russia Russland
Russian *(person)* russer(en)
  (adj) russisk

sad trist
safe trygg
safety pin sikkerhetsnål(en)
sailing boat seilbåt(en)
salad salat(en)
salami saltpølse(n)
sale *(at reduced prices)*
  salg(et)
salmon laks(en)
salt salt(et)

same samme
  the same people
  de samme menneskene
  same again, please
  samme igjen, takk
sand sand(en)
sandals sandaler
sandwich smørbrød(et)
sanitary towels damebind
satellite TV satelitt TV(en)
sauce saus(en)
saucepan kjele(n)
sauna badstue(n)
sausage pølse(n)
say si
  what did you say?
  hva sa du?
  how do you say ...?
  hvordan sier man ...?
Scandinavia Skandinavia
Scandinavian skandinavisk
scarf skjerf(et)
  (head) hodetørkle(et)
school skole(n)
scissors saks(en)
Scotland Skottland
Scotsman, Scotswoman skotte(n)
Scottish skotsk
screw skrue(n)
screwdriver skrutrekker(en)
sea sjø(en)
seafood fiskemat(en)
  (shellfish) skalldyr(et)
seat plass(en)
seat belt sikkerhetsbelte(t)
second *(of time)* sekund(et)
  (in series) annen
see se
  I can't see jeg kan ikke se
  I see *(understand)* jeg forstår
sell selge
separate separat
  (verb) skille

separated (*couple*) separert
serious alvorlig
serviette serviett(en)
several flere
sew sy
shampoo sjampo(en)
shave: to have a shave barberes
shaving foam barberskum(met)
shawl sjal(et)
she hun
sheet (*bed*) laken(et)
  (*paper*) ark(et)
shell skjell(et)
sherry sherry(en)
ship skip(et)
shirt skjorte(n)
shoelaces skolisser
shoe polish skokrem(en)
shoes sko
shop butikk(en)
shop (*verb*) handle
  to go shopping handle
short kort
shorts shorts
shoulder skulder(en)
shower (*bath*) dusj(en)
  (*rain*) regnskur(en)
shower gel dusj sepe(n)
shrimp reke(n)
shutter (*camera*) lukker(en)
  (*window*) vinduslem(men)
sick (*ill*) syk
  I feel sick jeg er kvalm
  to be sick kaste opp
side (*edge*) side(n)
  I'm on her side
  jeg er på hennes side
sidelights parkeringslys
sights: the sights of Oslo
  Oslos severdigheter
silk silke(n)
silver (*colour, metal*) sølv
simple enkel

sing synge
single (*one*) enkelt
  (*unmarried*) ugift
single room enkeltrom(met)
sister søster(en)
ski (*verb*) gå på ski
ski bindings bindinger
ski boots skistøvler
skid (*verb*) skli
skiing skigåing(en)
skin cleanser rensekrem(en)
ski resort skisenter(et)
skirt skjørt(et)
skis ski
ski sticks skistaver
sky himmel(en)
sleep (*noun*) søvn(en)
  (*verb*) sove
  to go to sleep sovne
sleeping bag sovepose(n)
sleeping pill sovepille(n)
slippers tøfler
slow sakte
small liten
smell (*noun*) lukt(en)
  (*verb*) lukte
smile (*noun*) smil(et)
  (*verb*) smile
smoke (*noun*) røyk(en)
  (*verb*) røyke
snack smårett(en)
snorkel snorkel(en)
snow snø(en)
so: so good så godt
  not so much ikke så mye
soaking solution (*for contact lenses*)
  desinfiseringsvæske(n)
socks sokker
soda water sodavann
soft (contact) lenses myke linser
somebody noen
somehow på en eller annen måte
something noe

sometimes noen ganger
somewhere et sted
son sønn(en)
song sang(en)
sorry: sorry! om forlatelse!
 I'm sorry om forlatelse
 sorry? *(pardon?)* hva?
soup suppe(n)
south syd, sør
South Africa Syd Afrika
South African *(person)* sydafrikaner
 (adj) sydafrikansk
souvenir suvenir(en)
spade *(shovel)* spade(n)
 (cards) spar
spanner skiftenøkkel(en)
spares reservedeler
spark(ing) plug tennplugg(en)
speak snakke
 do you speak …?
 snakker du …?
 I don't speak …
 jeg snakker ikke …
speed fart(en)
speed limit fartsgrense(n)
speedometer speedometer(et)
spider edderkopp(en)
spinach spinat(en)
spoon skje(en)
sprain senestrekk(et)
spring *(mechanical)* fjær(en)
 (season) vår(en)
square firkantet
 (street) plass(en)
stadium stadion(et)
staircase trapp(en)
stairs trapper
stamp frimerke(t)
stapler stiftemaskin(en)
star stjerne(n)
 (film) filmstjerne(n)
start *(verb)* starte
station stasjon(en)

statue statue(n)
stave church stavkirke(n)
steak biff(en)
steal stjele
 it's been stolen den er blitt stjålet
steering wheel ratt(et)
stewardess *(air)* flyvertinne(n)
sticky tape tape(n)
sting *(noun)* stikk(et)
 (verb) stikke
 it stings det svir
stockings strømper
stomach mage(n)
stomachache vondt i magen
stop *(verb)* stoppe
 (bus stop) buss-stopp(et)
 stop! stopp!
storm storm(en)
strawberry jordbær(et)
stream *(small river)* bekk(en)
street gate(n)
string *(cord)* hyssing(en)
 (guitar etc) streng(en)
student student(en)
stupid dum
suburb forstad(en)
sugar sukker(et)
suit *(noun: man's)* dress(en)
 (woman's) drakt(en)
 (verb) passe
 it suits you den kler deg
suitcase koffert(en)
sun sol(en)
sunbathe sole seg
sunburnt solbrent
sunglasses solbriller
sunny: it's sunny today
 det er sol i dag
suntan: to get a suntan bli brun
suntan lotion solkrem(en)
suntanned brun
supermarket supermarked(et)
supplement bilag(et)

123

sure sikker
  are you sure? er du sikker?
surname etternavn(et)
sweat *(noun)* svette(n)
  (verb) svette
sweatshirt genser(en)
Swede svenske(n)
Sweden Sverige
Swedish svensk
sweet *(not sour)* søt
  (candy) sukkertøy(et)
swim *(verb)* svømme
swimming: to go swimming bade
swimming costume badedrakt(en)
swimming pool svømmebasseng(et)
swimming trunks badebukse(n)
Swiss *(person)* sveitser(en)
  (adj) sveitsisk
switch bryter(en)
Switzerland Sveits
synagogue synagoge(n)

table bord(et)
tablet tablett(en)
take ta
takeoff *(noun)* start(en)
  (verb) starte
talcum powder talkum(en)
talk *(noun)* snakk(et)
  (verb) snakke
tall høy
tampons tampong(en)
tangerine mandarin(en)
tap kran(en)
tapestry korsstingsbroderi(et)
tea te(en)
tea towel oppvaskhåndkle(et)
telegram telegram(met)
telephone *(noun)* telefon(en)
  (verb) ringe
telephone box telefonkiosk(en)
telephone call telefonsamtale(n)

television fjernsyn(et)
temperature temperatur(en)
tent telt(et)
tent peg teltplugg(en)
tent pole teltstang(en)
than enn
thank *(verb)* takke
  thank you takk
  many thanks tusen takk
that: that bus/man/woman
  den bussen/mannen/damen
that: what's that? hva er det?
  I think that … jeg tror at …
their: their room rommet deres
  their books bøkene deres
  it's theirs det er deres
them: it's them det er dem
  it's for them det er til dem
  give it to them gi det til dem
then da
there *(place)* der
  there is/there are … det er …
  is there/are there …? er det …?
thermos flask termosflaske(n)
these: these things disse tingene
  these are mine disse er mine
they de
thick tykk
thin tynn
think tro, tenke
  I think so jeg tror det
  I'll think about it
  jeg skal tenke på det
third tredje
thirsty: I'm thirsty jeg er tørst
this: this bus/man/woman
  denne bussen/mannen/damen
  what's this? hva er dette?
  this is … dette er …
those: those things de tingene der
  those are his de er hans
throat hals(en)
throat pastilles halspastiller

through gjennom
thunderstorm tordenvær(et)
ticket billett(en)
tie (noun) slips(et)
  (verb) knyte
tights strømpebukse(n)
time tid(en)
  what's the time?
  hva er klokken?
timetable rutetabell(en)
tin boks(en)
tin opener hermetikkåpner(en)
tip (money) tips(et)
  (end) spiss(en)
tired trett
  I feel tired jeg er trett
tissues papirhåndkle(et)
to: to England til England
  to the station til stasjonen
  to the bank i banken
  to the cinema på kino
toast ristet brød
tobacco tobakk(en)
today i dag
together sammen
toilet toalett(et)
toilet paper toalettpapir(et)
tomato tomat(en)
tomato juice tomatjuice(n)
tomorrow i morgen
tongue tunge(n)
tonic water tonic
tonight i kveld
too (also) også
  (excessive) altfor
tooth tann(en)
toothache tannverk(en)
toothbrush tannbørste(n)
toothpaste tannkrem(en)
torch lommelykt(en)
tour rundtur(en)
tourist turist(en)
tourist office turistkontor(et)

towel håndkle(et)
tower tårn(et)
town by(en)
town hall rådhus(et)
toy leke(n)
toy shop leketøysbutikk(en)
track suit treningsdrakt(en)
tractor traktor(en)
tradition tradisjon(en)
traffic trafikk(en)
traffic jam trafikkork(en)
traffic lights trafikklys
trailer tilhenger(en)
train tog(et)
trainers joggesko
translate oversette
transmission (for car) overføring(en)
travel agency reisebyrå(et)
traveller's cheque reisesjekk(en)
tray brett(et)
tree tre(et)
troll troll(et)
trousers bukser
trout
  (freshwater) ferskvanns-ørret(en)
  (saltwater) sjø-ørret(en)
try prøve
tunnel tunnel(en)
tweezers pinsett(en)
typewriter skrivemaskin(en)
tyre dekk(et)

umbrella paraply(en)
uncle onkel(en)
under under
underground undergrunn(en)
underpants underbukse(n)
underskirt underskjørt(et)
understand forstå
  I don't understand
  jeg forstår ikke
underwear undertøy(et)

university universitet(et)
unleaded blyfri
unmarried ugift
until til
unusual uvanlig
up opp
  (*upwards*) oppover
urgent: it's urgent det haster
us: it's us det er oss
  it's for us det er til oss
  give it to us gi det til oss
use (*noun*) bruk(en)
  (*verb*) bruke
  it's no use det nytter ikke
useful nyttig
usual vanlig
usually vanligvis

vacancy (*room*) ledig rom
vacuum cleaner støvsuger(en)
vacuum flask termosflaske(n)
valley dal(en)
valve ventil(en)
vanilla vanilje
vase vase(n)
veal kalvekjøtt(et)
vegetable grønnsak(en)
vegetarian (*noun*) vegetarianer(en)
vehicle kjøretøy(et)
very veldig
vest trøye(n)
video video(en)
video tape video kassett(en)
view utsikt(en)
viewfinder søker(en)
Viking viking(en)
  Viking ship vikingskip(et)
villa villa(en)
village landsby(en)
vinegar eddik(en)
violin fiolin(en)
visa visum(et)

visit (*noun*) besøk(et)
  (*verb*) besøke
visitor gjest(en)
  (*tourist*) turist(en)
vitamin tablet vitaminpille(n)
vodka vodka(en)
voice stemme(n)

wait (*verb*) vente
  wait! vent!
waiter kelner(en)
  waiter! kelner!
waiting room venterom(met)
waitress serveringsdame(n)
  waitress! hallo!
Wales Wales
walk (*noun: stroll*) tur(en)
  (*verb*) gå
  to go for a walk gå en tur
wall (*house*) vegg(en)
wallet lommebok(en)
war krig(en)
wardrobe garderobeskap(et)
warm varm
was: I was jeg var
  he/she/it was han/hun/det var
washing powder vaskepulver(et)
washing-up liquid oppvaskmiddel(et)
wasp veps(en)
watch (*noun*) klokke(n)
  (*verb*) se
water vann(et)
waterfall foss(en)
wave (*noun: sea*) bølge(n)
  (*verb: goodbye*) vinke
we vi
weather vær(et)
Web site web side(n)
wedding bryllup(et)
week uke(n)
welcome velkommen
  you're welcome! bare hyggelig!

wellingtons gummistøvler
Welsh walisisk
Welshman, Welshwoman waliser(en)
were: we were vi var
  you were (*singular*) du var
  (*plural*) dere var
  they were de var
west vest
wet våt
what? hva?
wheel hjul(et)
wheelchair rullestol(en)
when? når?
where? hvor?
whether om
which? hvilken?
whisky whisky(en)
white hvit
who? hvem?
why? hvorfor?
wide bred
wife kone(n)
wind vind(en)
window vindu(et)
windscreen frontrute(n)
wine vin(en)
wine list vinkart(et)
wing vinge(n)
with med
without uten
woman kvinne(n)
women (*toilet*) damer, kvinner
wood (*material*) tre(et)
  (*forest*) skog(en)

wool ull(en)
word ord(et)
work (*noun*) arbeid(et)
  (*verb*) arbeide
worse verre
worst verst
wrapping paper innpakningspapir(et)
wrist håndledd(et)
writing paper skrivepapir(et)
wrong feil

year år(et)
yellow gul
yes ja
yesterday i går
yet ennå
  not yet ikke ennå
yoghurt yoghurt(en)
you (*singular*) du
  (*plural*) dere
your: your book (*singular*) din bok
  (*plural*) deres bok
  your shoes (*singular*) dine sko
  (*plural*) deres sko
yours: is this yours?
  (*singular*) er denne din?
  (*plural*) er denne deres?
youth hostel
  vandrerhjem(met)

zip glidelås(en)
zoo dyrehage(n)